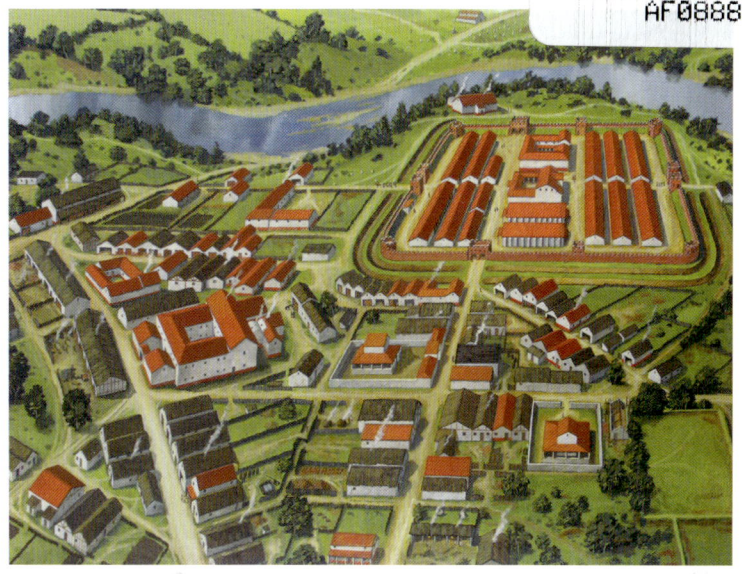

THE ORIGINS OF MANCHESTER

ROMAN CONQUEST TO INDUSTRIAL REVOLUTION

ALAN KIDD

For my grandchildren,
Alex, Max and Theo, with love

Acknowledgements

Anyone who sets out to write a general history risks treading on several toes; one cannot have specialist knowledge in every area. I have been fortunate in the assistance and advice I have received from others especially those who commented on the text in preparation: Alistair Hodge, Terry Wyke and Norman Redhead. However, any errors the reader may find are entirely my own doing. I am also grateful to the several institutions which gave permission to publish the archive illustrations that accompany the text and to Anna Goddard who took most of the photographs and to Ian Reid who drew the new maps.

First published in 2023

by Carnegie Publishing
Carnegie House
Chatsworth Road
Lancaster LA1 4SL
www.carnegiepublishing.com

Copyright © Alan Kidd

All rights reserved
Unauthorised duplication contravenes existing laws
The right of Alan Kidd to be identified as the author of this work has been asserted in accordance with the Copyright, Designs and Patents act 1988

British Library Cataloguing-in-Publication data
A catalogue record for this book is available from the British Library
Every effort has been made to trace copyright holders.

Paperback ISBN 13: 978-1-85936-239-6

Designed and typeset by Carnegie Book Production
www.carnegiebookproduction.com
Printed and bound by Cambrian Printers

Contents

	Preface	iv
	Introduction	1
1	Mamucium: a Roman fort	3
2	Mamecestre: a medieval market town	15
3	'The fairest, best builded, quikkest and most populous tounne of al Lancastreshire': Manchester 1543–1660	34
4	'The greatest mere village in England': roots of industrial revolution, 1660–1780	61
5	Living in eighteenth-century Manchester	82
	Notes and references	116
	Index	121

Preface

It is now almost thirty years since the first edition of my history of Manchester was published. This was one of a series of town and city histories published by Ryburn that focused on modern urban history, especially the industrial revolution and after. The text was revised in subsequent editions but the focus remained the last two centuries. While the industrial era was undoubtedly the period when Manchester strode the global stage and played a leading role in world history, I have long felt the need to provide a history of the origins of Manchester, a city whose recorded past stretches back almost 2,000 years. The book you are holding in your hands is the result. It gives me an opportunity to take the story of Manchester back to its beginnings both to study the past in its own right but also to seek the roots of Manchester's remarkable modern history. Here you will find chapters on the Roman fort, medieval Manchester, the sixteenth and seventeenth centuries, and two chapters on the under-studied but crucial eighteenth century. I hope readers who are familiar with my earlier book will find much to interest them here and that new readers will be attracted by a history that explores Manchester's past during the many centuries preceding the industrial revolution.

This history has been written with a broad readership in mind: local people interested to know how their town has evolved over time; newcomers and visitors curious to acquire an historical introduction to their new surroundings and the student and scholar seeking to understand the roots of the modern world. With these potential audiences in mind the book has been informed by research and scholarship but written as accessibly as possible in the hope of bringing that historical scholarship to a wide readership.

A study of an historically important place such as Manchester needs no justification, but it may seem curious to some that this is a history of Manchester alone and not also of its close neighbour, Salford. However, a compelling reason for treating Manchester and Salford separately is their quite distinct political identities and independent traditions of urban pride, both of which have their origins in the pre-industrial period.[1]

Introduction

Every town and city has its story, but few have a history which belongs to the world. Manchester was arguably the first world's modern city. Changes wrought by the industrial revolution caused unprecedented urban growth, ushered in new ways of living and working, and generated new ideas of economy and society. What happened here offered a model that was imitated across the world.

But, however important those events were, the history of Manchester did not begin with steam-powered factories and industrial canals. The first Manchester was a civil settlement that gathered outside the gates of a frontier fort at the remote edge of the Roman empire. The remains of this fort can be seen today in Castlefield. Several centuries after the Romans left, Manchester was fortified again, this time in defence against Viking raiders. The buildings of the medieval town huddled around a Norman castle on the site of today's Chetham's School of Music. The political origins of the separation of Manchester from Salford lie in the era following the Norman Conquest and this teaches us how deep rooted are some of our modern divisions and traditions. As more peaceful centuries ensued, a market town developed and gradually grew into one of the leading towns in the north-west of England. By the sixteenth century Manchester was catching the eye of travellers and writers, and its place in the narrative of the nation's history had begun. From this time until the first steam-powered factories appeared in the last decade of the eighteenth century the roots of later greatness were laid down. This book will ask how significant were the centuries before the industrial revolution in helping us to understand that event of world significance.

Although the centuries preceding the industrial revolution are interesting for the light they can throw on Manchester's role in that momentous occurrence, the history of the town during this era has the power to surprise us. For example, Mancunians played their part in the dramatic events of the English Civil War of the 1640s that pitted opposing parliamentarian and royalist forces and which was to culminate in the execution of the king.

Manchester was the site of one of early skirmishes of the civil war, and pitched battles took place on its streets and squares for several days. In this contest Manchester was for the parliament against the Stuart king, Charles I. Yet less than a century later the town earned the reputation of being a Jacobite stronghold, a supporter of the Stuart pretenders to the throne (the last Stuart monarch, James II, had been ejected by parliament in 1688) against the legitimacy of the Hanoverian monarchs. In particular Manchester gave direct succour to the Stuart cause in the Jacobite rising of 1745 when rebel forces were welcomed into the town including the 'Young Pretender', Bonnie Prince Charlie, himself. As a result after the defeat of the Jacobite rebellion the town was put under military occupation by government troops. It took some time before the taint of treason could be erased from the town's image. Nonetheless, it was during these two centuries that the nation came to recognise Manchester's identity as a trading town and even before the first factory was built cotton goods were being sent round the globe from Manchester warehouses.

During the nineteenth century Manchester was to become one of the most famous cities in the world: a pivotal site of the first industrial revolution and the greatest of the trading cities created by that revolution. This is the period in the history of the city that is most well-known. Yet the long history of Manchester from Roman fort, through the medieval and early modern eras up to the crucial but little researched eighteenth century that lay the foundations for the industrial revolution is less well understood. It is hoped that this book will be a useful contribution to recovering and appreciating that history, and to understanding the origins of Manchester.

1

Mamucium: a Roman fort

It is quite easy to live or work in the Manchester of today and be completely unaware that the history of this great modern city began with the Roman occupation of Britain, two thousand years ago. Manchester is situated just south-west of the foothills of the Pennines, with the Cheshire plain to the south. This undulating glacial landscape long ago carved out the natural defences and provided the navigable rivers which attracted the earliest settlers. The casual visitor to modern Manchester could be excused, however, for failing to notice that the city centre occupies the land where one large river, the Irwell, meets two smaller streams, the Irk and the Medlock. Urban development has obscured the natural geography of the place. It also hides the fact that there have been two 'Manchesters' in the past: a medieval town on the high ground above the confluence of the Irwell and the Irk, the area around the present-day cathedral, and a Roman fort a little farther down river where the Medlock flows into the Irwell, in what is now Castlefield. Thus the modern visitor who passes along Deansgate from one end to the other is following a thoroughfare linking medieval 'Mamecestre' to Roman 'Mamucium'.

The first Manchester – Roman Mamucium – consisted of a military fort and civil settlement on the remote northern edge of the vast Roman Empire. The fort was placed strategically at a meeting point between two important Roman roads: an east–west route climbing high across the Pennines linking the chief legionary bases of northern Britannia, *Eboracum* (York) and *Deva* (Chester), and another route striking north along the western rim of the Pennines to *Luguvalium* (Carlisle) and the frontier with the Picts at Hadrian's Wall. Among several other roads connected to the Roman fort at Manchester was a link to neighbouring *Coccium* (Wigan) and a route south-eastwards into the Peak District, where valuable mineral resources had been discovered. In addition to these, there was a number of other routes: Mamucium's location was crucial for both military and trading lines of communication.

'Mamucium' is the generally accepted name for the Roman settlement; it may be a Latinised version of a Celtic word, *mam*, meaning 'breast' which is often found in ancient hill names (such as Mam Tor in Derbyshire). That being said, we cannot be certain what the Romans called it: some have suggested Mammium, although Mancunium is now thought unlikely.[1] When the Romans came, the broad swath from the northern Peak District to Hadrian's Wall, and including at least part of the Manchester basin, was the homeland of a loosely confederated Celtic tribe, which the Romans called the Brigantes. They were Iron Age peoples, mainly pastoralists although

Mamucium in 200AD A bird's-eye view of how the Roman fort and settlement may have looked in around 200 AD when Emperor Severus visited. (Artist's impression by Graham Sumner, based on advice from Norman Redhead)

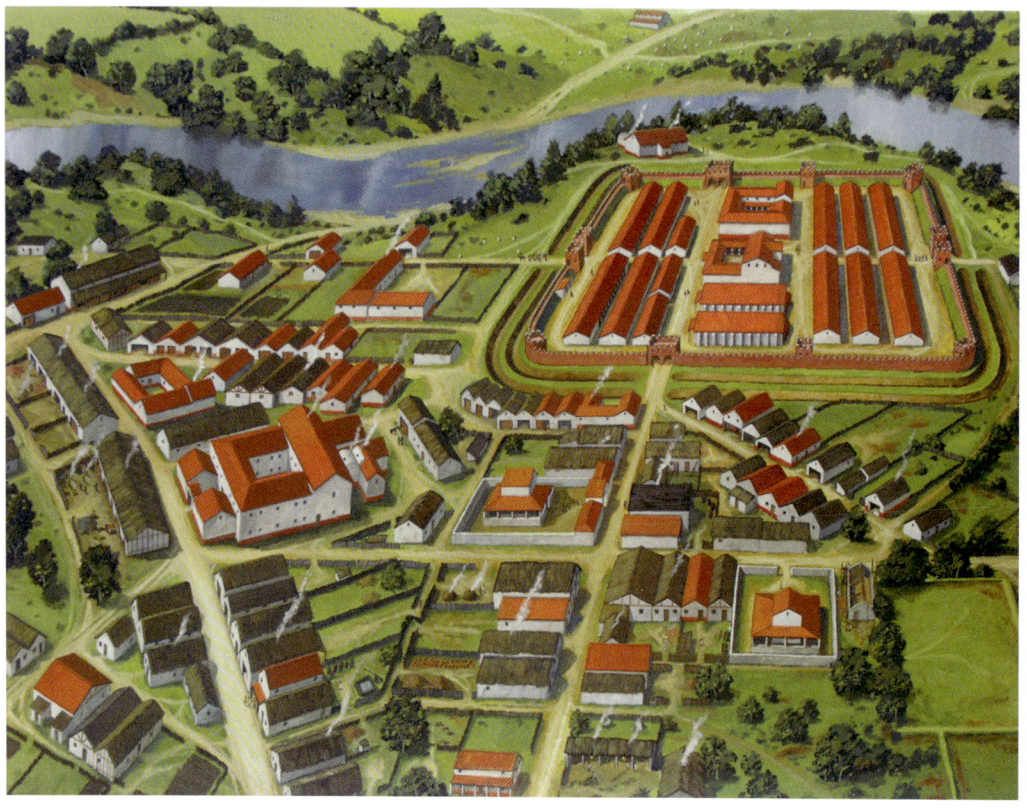

they also worked metal and made pottery. Almost nothing is known of the smaller groups within this confederation, though some have suggested that in the Manchester region there may have been a sub-group called the Setantii. Lands to the south – the Cheshire plain and present-day Shropshire – were part of the territory of the Cornovii. This means that Mamucium was situated close to the boundary between two great tribal groupings. This may have been important for trade, as well as being of strategic significance.

The Roman conquest of Britain began in AD 43 and by 59 the tribes of the South, the Midlands and much of Wales were under Roman rule as the province of Britannia. Some time during this period (according to the Roman historian, Tacitus) the Brigantes, under their queen, Cartimandua, acted as a 'client' state, which meant the Romans did not have to worry about their northern flank in their conquest of the tribes of the South and the West. However, by AD 69 Brigantian power had fallen to Cartimandua's husband, Venetius, who opposed the alliance with Rome. The Romans soon moved to subdue their unstable former ally. In the 70s two Roman governors, Quintis Petilius Cerialis and Gnaius Julius Agricola, undertook campaigns against the Brigantes and other northern tribes. The conquest of Brigantia therefore took place in the mid-70s, as a result of the civil war which had brought an anti-Roman ruler to power. For decades thereafter Brigantian territory was under direct military rule and its forts were therefore vital to the control of the region.

Following the account in Tacitus it is generally accepted that Agricola, the new governor, conducted military operations west of the Pennines. Tacitus tells us that Agricola personally selected the sites for his forts and given its strategic importance it is reasonable to conclude that this included Mamucium. The fort at Mamucium was located on a rocky outcrop in a loop of the river Medlock, east of its confluence with the Irwell. The earliest Roman levels excavated by archaeologists date from about AD 77–78, and military occupation of the site lasted for well over three hundred years, possibly until the Romans left Britain early in the fifth century. Today, physical evidence for the fort has been mostly obliterated by developments during the industrial revolution. First, in 1760 the construction of the Bridgewater Canal destroyed the bath house and in 1804 the Rochdale Canal cut a diagonal line right through the site. Later the building of the railway viaduct leading west from Central Station (Manchester Central Convention Complex) caused further damage to the site. The remainder of the fort lies under the foundations of nineteenth-century buildings and roads. Its location can be discovered off the southern end of Deansgate via Castle Street, where the visitor can see a full-size reconstruction of the twin-portalled northern gateway as it may have appeared in the third century and three buildings of the civilian settlement (*vicus*) marked out on the ground, in gardens opposite the former Air and Space Hall of the Museum of Science and Industry. Nearby, off Duke Place, a section of the defensive wall just north of where the west gate was located has also been reconstructed, with the location of a granary marked out on the ground.

Our knowledge of this, the earliest settlement of Manchester, is based partly on documentary sources written by observers who saw the remains of the fort up to the eighteenth century but chiefly on the work of archaeologists in more recent times. There have been several excavations at the Castlefield site since the eighteenth century, including detailed work in the 1970s on the northern and western defences.[2] These excavations found extensive evidence for successive building phases beginning in the late first century and continuing into the early third century. They revealed that the first fort on the site was square in plan, covering about three acres and designed to hold a 480-man infantry unit. Inscription evidence uncovered by archaeologists suggests this unit may have been composed of soldiers drawn from from modern-day Germany, Austria and Hungary. This original fort of timber with defensive turf ramparts and ditches was renovated and strengthened around the end of the first century. Outer pits covered with brushwood, in which upturned sharpened stakes were concealed, may have supplemented the defensive ditches that surrounded the fort. These would have proved hazardous 'mantraps' in the event of an assault. Indeed, there is evidence that around the middle of the second century the ramparts were seriously damaged and the defensive wall burned down. Archaeologists are confident the evidence points to a wholesale demolition and abandonment of the fort. Does this mean it was destroyed in a Brigantian uprising? Did a great, but unrecorded, battle take place here? Northern Britain was always difficult territory for the Romans and the military garrisons had to maintain a constant 'policing' role. Certainly the early second century was a tense and dangerous period, but the real military problems lay elsewhere, in Scotland. It seems most likely that the fort at Mamucium was decommissioned as troops were moved north, following the decision in the AD 140s of the Emperor Antoninus Pius to occupy southern Scotland. However, it may have been in response to a Brigantian revolt that the Romans decided to renew their fort on the river Medlock around AD 160. We know that a new timber fort was built at this time. The new oblong structure was larger than its predecessor, covering five acres and with stronger ramparts and gates, and was probably

Reconstructed Gateway of the Roman Fortress The final stage in the fort's defensive evolution came around the year 200 when timber walls and gateways were rebuilt in stone. It is this third-century gateway that is reconstructed on the site today.
(Image © Carnegie Publishing)

designed to house a mixed force of 480 infantry and 128 cavalry with a correspondingly larger granary.³

The final stage in the fort's defensive evolution came around the year 200 when timber defences and gateways were rebuilt in stone. The third-century gateway is the one that is reconstructed on the site today. This stone-built fort continued in use for another two hundred years, until the end of the Roman presence in the early fifth century. Ironically it may have been after the second century that hostility to the occupation finally waned. Although stone may be regarded a better defence than timber, during the third and fourth centuries Mamucium was probably regarded as a peaceful posting for the Roman military. The third-century stone gateway perhaps had a largely

Roman Stone Altar discovered in 1612 Mithras was a very popular god with Roman soldiers and merchants. An altar stone was found in 1612 beside the River Medlock which was dedicated to Fortune the Preserver by Lucius Senicianius Martius. He was a legionary commander detached to Manchester from the VIth Legion in York and may have been responsible for rebuilding the fort defences in 200 AD. (Photograph by Mike Peel)

8   Mamucium: a Roman fort

symbolic role as an emblem of Roman power, rather than as an unassailable mechanism of defence. In peaceful times it had most to do with the regulation of civilian traffic in and out of the fort. Much of this traffic would have been trade related, for Mamucium's location at the hub of the regional transport network means that it was certainly a trading centre.[4] Roman coinage was first introduced directly into the region in the AD 50s and 60s, a result of military rather than commercial activity. However, the presence of the Roman army from the 70s onwards provided an enlarged market for imported goods and the monetary currency to encourage trade.

The first Manchester

Although the Brigantes were never fully integrated into the Roman Empire and the military function of Mamucium remained its ultimate *raison d'être*, a civil settlement, or *vicus*, grew up outside the fort walls. All Roman forts occupied for any considerable length of time developed such settlements.[5] In peaceful conditions they might develop into the towns and cities of the Roman occupation, although this was rare in the North. In contrast to the more important Roman towns, such as Cirencester or Wroxeter, they were not planned but instead developed haphazardly over time in response to need. Generally they provided facilities for the troops and housed small industrial workshops. They also acted as market places where local farmers sold their produce and traders dealt in manufactured wares and consumer goods. Archaeological excavation of the Roman *vici* in Britain lags behind the work that has been done on military fortifications. However, Manchester is one of the few sites where there has been extensive investigation of the civil settlement. As a result we know that the *vicus* at Mamucium occupied the high ground on the northern bank of the river Medlock and extended to the southern bank of the river opposite the south-eastern corner of the fort. Most of the area to the south and west was marshy and waterlogged, and unsuitable for habitation. Outside the fort's northern gateway, basic timber-frame houses faced the occasional more substantial two-storey structure, overlooking surrounding market gardens. Iron-working furnaces abutted storehouses, workshops and brothels. Building designs were typically rectangular, although some had verandas, while others were in the form of a shed open along one side, and there were also U-shaped complexes around central yards. There is some evidence that the timber-framed buildings were supported on low walls made of stone.[6]

This was the first 'Manchester'. What went on here? The evidence indicates that it was primarily an industrial site, in which large-scale iron working took place under military control. In fact, the body of archaeological evidence accumulated over the past fifty years suggests that Manchester was the most important industrial *vicus* in the region, functioning almost as an 'industrial estate' and supply depot servicing other forts. Over thirty furnaces and smithing hearths were found during excavations in the 1970s. These may have been used to fashion imported iron blooms into weapons and tools, and other equipment including hobnails for the soldiers leather footwear.[7]

As well as evidence of industrial activity the archaeological record has yielded some interesting details about the beliefs of the occupants of Roman Manchester.[8] Finds include objects and inscriptions that illustrate official and unofficial Roman religions and perhaps even provide the earliest evidence for

Roman Stone Altar discovered in 2008 This is an extraordinary glimpse of what may still lie beneath our feet. A well-preserved Roman altar was found in a pit close to Chester Road on the south side of the River Medlock. The one metre-tall stone was erected on the approach to Mamucium by a soldier called Aelius Victor. It is dedicated to the goddesses Henaneftis and Ollototis from Celtic tribes in the Rhineland area of Germany, so Aelius may have been conscripted there and posted to Mamucium. The inscription on the altar reads: DEABUS MATRIBUS HANANEFTIS ET OLLOTOTIS AELIUS VICTOR V.S.L.L.M [v(otum) s(olvit) l(aetus) l(ibens) m(erito)] *To the mother goddesses, the Hananeftae and the Ollototae, Aelius Victor gladly, willingly and deservedly fulfilled his vow.* (Photograph by Norman Redhead)

Manchester Word Square A fragment of broken pottery incised with Latin letters was found during an excavation of the site of the Roman fort in the 1970s. The writing on this potsherd, ROTAS OPERA, was very similar to better preserved word squares that had Christian connotations found in different parts of the Roman Empire. The completed word square would have read: ROTAS OPERA TENET AREPO SATOR or 'Arepo the sower guides the wheels with care'. This appeared to be nonsense until the lettering is read as a kind of code and the words PATERNOSTER or 'our father' revealed. The unused letters were A and O or alpha and omega – again charged with Christian meaning. Inscriptions like this were used to identify fellow-believers at a time when the Christian religion was being persecuted by the Roman authorities. The stratigraphic location of the potsherd in the civilian settlement attached to the fort gives this the very precise date of 182 AD. If this is a Christian artefact it is one of the earliest examples of Christianity in Roman Britain. Pictured here is a terracotta replica of the completed word square. (Image courtesy of the Manchester Museum, the University of Manchester)

Christian worship in the North West. The Roman authorities required some forms of religious observance, and surviving altars and dedications record loyalty to the emperor or to the gods (sometimes the two being more or less synonymous). As long ago as 1612 a stone altar which had been dedicated to 'Fortune the Preserver' by a centurion of the Sixth Legion was found 'under the roote of an oak in Medlock neere Knott Mill'. As recently as 2008 another altar was uncovered on the southern side of Chester Road near the river Medlock. This last find is remarkably complete, and the dedication

Jupiter Stator statuette found in 1839 Jupiter was one of the most powerful gods in the Roman pantheon. This bronze statue mounted on a removable base was found while laying the foundations for a building in Tonman Street, Manchester.
(Image courtesy of Manchester Art Gallery)

reveals it had been set up by a man called Aelius Victor in honour of the mother goddesses of a Germanic tribe, the Cannanefates, who lived at the mouth of the river Rhine. He is very likely to have been a German who was recruited into the Roman army and posted to Mamucium some time in the second century AD. Less common survivals are the smaller metal or pottery items designed for display in the purchaser's own home. A popular devotional subject was the god, Jupiter, chief deity in the Roman pantheon (*Jupiter Optimus Maximus*). In 1839 while the foundations were being dug for the Hall of Science in Tonman Street, Campfield (later to house Manchester Free Library) a bronze statuette of Jupiter was discovered. Standing 5¼ inches

(13.5 cm) in height, the statuette was complete with thunderbolts of Jove in one hand and a rod in the other. Unfortunately these, together with the pedestal were soon, unaccountably, lost. Excavations in the early twenty-first century revealed a temple site complete with a cremation burial urn, although it is unclear which deity was being venerated.

As well as official and semi-official deities, there is local evidence of certain of the Roman 'mystery' cults notably Mithraism and possibly Christianity. No Mithraic temples are known within the North West, but it is likely that Mithraic worship was conducted on at least an occasional basis at most military sites. It has been long presumed there were such practices in Roman Manchester. In 1821 workmen sinking a drain in Hulme, to the south of the fort site, uncovered a block of stone on which was carved the figure of a man dressed in a tunic with his left leg crossed before the right and a Persian cap on his head. In his right hand was a torch pressed downwards into the

Mithraic stone found in Hulme 1821 This depicts Cautopates, one of the torch-bearers attending the god Mithras, and has the usual form of crossed legs and the torch held downwards. The figure stands within a raised square border or moulding. The lower moulding on one side suggests that it was part of a series. (Photograph by Mike Peel)

ground while the left hand supported his chin. The broken edge of the panel showed that it had formed the extreme right wing of a series. The figure can be identified as Cautopates, an important accessory figure connected with the worship of the Persian god Mithras, which had followers among soldiers and merchants.[9]

The evidence for Mithraism in the vicinity of Mamucium is thus fairly clear. Less certain is that for early Christianity, which was a forbidden religion until Constantine's Edict of Milan of 312. However, a tantalising if ambiguous find from the 1970s' excavations has been interpreted as possible evidence of Christian worship. A fragment of amphora (wine container) inscribed with part of a 'word square' seems to have letters that can be re-arranged to give the words PATER NOSTER (meaning 'Our Father') (twice) with two spare As and Os (Alpha and Omega – the beginning and the end). The letters of the square allow the words to be arranged in a cruciform fashion. This dates to the second century, before Christianity was legal, and if authentic would be the oldest Christian artefact in the North West and one of the earliest examples of Christianity in Britain. Although scholars have concluded that this find may not have a Christian significance it remains an intriguing and mysterious survival.[10]

The Manchester *vicus* declined considerably during the third century despite coin finds and other evidence demonstrating that the fort continued during this period. By the fourth century, a large outer ditch was dug outside the existing ditch system, cutting through the road to the northern gateway. This suggests the road was no longer in use and that the *vicus* may have disappeared completely. In any case it did not survive the Romans' departure from Britain. As at most other places in northern England, urban or semi-urban lifestyles quickly disappeared, and the Roman settlement itself was abandoned. The stone walls of the fort survived as an impressive ruin for centuries. Indeed, the fort itself was possibly briefly reoccupied five hundred years after the Romans left, as discussed below. The walls were then steadily plundered for building materials, but even as late as the early eighteenth century substantial remains could still be seen. Soon, however, the area on the north bank of the Medlock was to become a focus for intense industrial activity and today the great viaduct, which carries the main line west from Oxford Road and Deansgate stations, strides across the site of the Roman fort. All the archaeological evidence suggests that in the long centuries following the end of Mamucium the area became purely rural, with village settlements, and agriculture the only significant economic activity. The first Manchester was just a folk memory.

2

Mamecestre: a medieval market town

Her on þysum geare for Eadweard cyning mid fierde onufan hærfest to þelwæle, & het gewyrcan þa burg, & gesettan, & gemannian; & het oþre fierd eac of Miercna þeode þa hwile þe he þær sæt gefaran Mameceaster on Norþhymbrum, & hie gebetan & gemannian.

ANGLO-SAXON CHRONICLE, 923

Over five centuries after the Romans left, Manchester reappears in the historical record in a brief reference in the *Anglo-Saxon Chronicle* under the year 923: 'In this year after autumn King Edward went with the army to Thelwall and ordered the borough to be built, occupied and manned; and while he stayed there he ordered another army, also from the people of Mercia, to occupy Manchester in Northumbria, and repair and man it.'

This entry refers to an event in the military re-conquest of Viking England by the kings of Wessex, in this case Edward the Elder, son of Alfred the Great. The first recorded Viking raid in England had been on the monastery of Lindisfarne in 793. This was a precedent for over 80 years of coastal raids and territorial incursions that saw Scandinavian subjugation of the Anglo-Saxon kingdoms of Northumbria, Mercia and East Anglia, with Wessex alone remaining a centre of English resistance. Under Alfred the Great and his successors, armies from Wessex began the recovery of English lands. Although there were few towns or wealthy monasteries to attract

Viking raiders, north-west England became a focus of confrontation in the ninth and tenth centuries due to its strategic position between the Viking settlements at Dublin and York. Moreover, in the opening years of the tenth century Norwegian settlers poured into the North West after their expulsion from Dublin. In response to this, first Aethelflaed, Lady of the Mercians, and then her brother, Edward the Elder, borrowed an idea that had been tried and tested in their father's kingdom of Wessex, the building of fortified settlements or *burhs* to act as military bases from which to defend frontiers and reconquer territory. Aethelflaed and Edward built a chain of *burhs* along the northern frontier, from Rhuddlan and Chester along the Mersey to Manchester, and then to Bakewell in the east.

The *Anglo-Saxon Chronicle* entry implies the *re*fortification of Manchester rather than the building of an entirely new military base. It might be that an existing settlement had been taken or attacked by Viking raiders, but that we have no direct historical or archaeological confirmation. Indeed, there is little convincing archaeological evidence of occupation of the site in the centuries between the Roman era and this mention of Manchester in the tenth century: certainly not enough to suggest any form of continuous settlement.[1] However, some tentative archaeological finds support the idea of more settled occupation during the ninth and tenth centuries, notably coins of the period, although the 'Angel Stone', now in Manchester Cathedral and long thought to date from the tenth century, is now regarded as being of late-eleventh century date.[2]

We cannot even be sure of the precise location of the *burh* established in 923. The *Anglo-Saxon Chronicle* reference to the 'repair' of Manchester could mean the restoration of the old Roman fortifications, but while this remains entirely plausible, archaeological excavation has failed to provide conclusive evidence. The alternative location is at the other end of Deansgate, where Chetham's College and the Cathedral stand today. A concentration of Saxon coins has been found in this area and the case for this location is strengthened by the knowledge that this is where the medieval town of Manchester developed in the centuries following the Norman Conquest in 1066.[3] However, the use of the word 'repair' remains puzzling – what was there to repair at that location? As is apparent, our knowledge of this period in the town's past remains very hazy, but it is reasonable to assume a continuity of settlement in the Manchester area from the late-Saxon period onwards. Wherever it was located, Edward the Elder's *burh* resumed the line of occupation that had been broken by the departure of the Romans.

The name 'Manchester' does not appear in the written historical record again for more than a century and a half, which is unsurprising since documentary evidence is extremely scarce for the whole of North-West England in the tenth and early eleventh centuries. Even the Domesday survey of 1086, which is so valuable a source for the lands farther south, is terse and often ambiguous for the area that became Lancashire. William the Conqueror assessed the income and assets of his new kingdom and the reference to Manchester merely refers to lands held by the church, rather than to any township of Manchester.

Parish and manor of Manchester

King Edward [the Confessor] held Salford. There are three hides. And twelve carucates of land waste. And forest three miles long, and the same broad. And there are many hays and an aerie of hawks. King Edward held Radcliffe for a manor. There is one hide and another belonging to Salford. The church of St. Mary and the church of St. Michael held in Mamecestre one carucate of land quit from every due except geld.

DOMESDAY BOOK, 1086

The reference to Mamecestre in the Domesday Book could refer either to the parish of Manchester or to the manor of Manchester. However, we have to wait until the early thirteenth century for reliable documentary evidence of an urban settlement. The Domesday entry reveals that at the time of the survey the churches of St Mary and St Michael held land in Manchester. Most historians conclude, on the basis of their medieval dedications, that those churches were at Manchester and Ashton-under-Lyne respectively. Thus at the time of the Conquest Manchester already had a church. We know from later evidence that its parish was extensive. In the medieval period it covered about sixty square miles, and lay between the parish of Prestwich-cum-Oldham in the north, Ashton-under-Lyne and the river Tame to the east, with Flixton and Eccles in the west and the river Mersey from Stockport to Urmston to the south. It embraced over two dozen separate townships, including Denton, Blackley, Stretford, Heaton Norris, Didsbury and Salford.

At the time of the Domesday Book, it is likely that the land by the Irwell and the Irk we now know as Manchester was primarily agricultural in character. In 1086 the North West was a sparsely populated and backward part of the Conqueror's patrimony. In terms of its territorial organisation it bore the marks of the Saxon reconquest of the tenth century. There was not yet a county of Lancashire, and Manchester was within a territory of ambiguous status which Domesday labels 'inter Ripam et Mersham', the land between the Ribble and the Mersey. Edward the Elder had separated that area from Northumbria and from the diocese of York, and had joined it to the Mercian diocese of Lichfield. In the Domesday survey this land was assessed separately from the more remote region north of the Ribble. After the Conquest it had been divided into six divisions called hundreds or wapentakes, one of which was the hundred of Salford, which included Manchester.

Salford Hundred was one of the territories granted by a grateful William the Conqueror to his friend, close supporter and distant cousin Roger de Poitou (or Roger the Poitevin), who had been with him at the Battle of Hastings in 1066. By William's grant Roger was given all the land from the Mersey to the heart of the Lake District, and in turn divided this newly acquired area into a number of fiefdoms, among them the barony of Manchester. The first baron of Manchester was another Norman knight, Albert de Gresle (anglicised as 'Grelley') whose family ruled the manor of Manchester for two centuries. In the later Middle Ages it changed hands several times before coming to rest, in the 1590s, with the Mosley family who held the manor until the newly created Corporation of Manchester bought out the Mosley manorial rights in 1846.

Under the Grelleys the barony of Manchester included scattered estates in the hundreds of Leyland and West Derby but chiefly comprised the greater part of the north-western and south-eastern corners of the Hundred of Salford, including most of the parish of Manchester. Their lands were further divided into sub-baronies, whose local lords did service to their overlord of Manchester. In understanding the complexities of land ownership in this era it helps to distinguish between the lands of the barony of Manchester, which were extensive and geographically widespread, and the manor of Manchester in the specific sense of the Gresle lands which had not been granted out as sub-manors. Within the area of Manchester there were the three large and important sub-manors of Ashton-under-Lyne, Heaton Norris and Withington, while the rest formed the manor of Manchester proper. In 1322 this included up to 1,200 acres of arable, four acres of meadow and 86 acres of pasture. This was demesne land, retained for the lord's own use. In addition there were the lands held by freeholders, leaseholders and villeins, and also the common lands in which all had rights.[4] Most of the arable acres lay to the north and east, reclaimed from barren moorland and marshland.

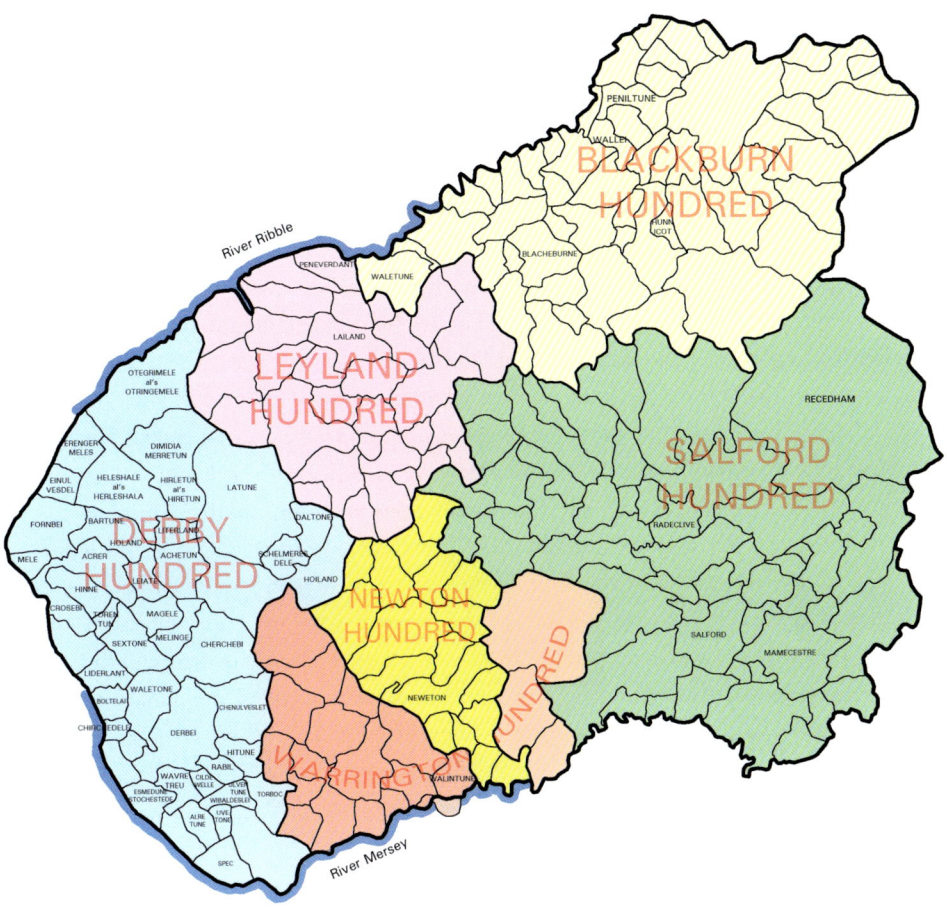

Land between the rivers Ribble and Mersey After the Norman Conquest this territory had been divided into six divisions called hundreds or wapentakes, one of which was the hundred of Salford, which included Manchester. This map shows the hundreds and places identified in the Domesday Book of 1086. (Image drawn by Ian Reid based on map in W. Farrer, 'Notes on the Domesday survey' *Transactions of the Lancashire & Cheshire Antiquarian Society*, XVI, 1898)

The ancient arable lands closest to the town lay between Deansgate and the Irwell and are today recalled in such names as Dolefield and Ridgefield.

At the physical heart of the post-Conquest manor of Manchester was a castle. Few people realise that Manchester once had a castle, which is not surprising since it was of no special political or military importance. It stood where Chetham's College stands today, on the flat summit of a sandstone bluff overlooking the confluence of the Irwell and the Irk. The castle was most probably a timber structure with an encircling wooden palisade. The first mention of the castle was in 1184 and it disappears from the historical record after the baronial revolt against King John in 1215, when Robert de Gresle was one of the barons who forced the king to sign the Magna Carta at Runnymede. In retribution the pope excommunicated him and the crown confiscated his lands, although these (along with the castle) were subsequently returned to him. We know that by the late thirteenth century the Grelleys had replaced the castle with a fortified manor house.

From their base in the castle, and its successor the manor house, the Grelleys as lords of the manor let out land to free and villein tenants who, in return, worked on the demesne land at required times. They held the fishing rights on the Irwell, and owned the town's mill, on the Irk at the end of the street which is still named Long Millgate. There all manorial tenants had to grind their corn. Today its site lies deeply buried beneath Victoria Station (under which the Irk now runs in a black and stygian tunnel). These were agricultural interests, but the lord of the manor of Manchester was also to benefit from the growing number of his tenants who were exempt from compulsory labour services and did not work on the land. As the town began to grow in the thirteenth and fourteenth centuries there were increasing numbers of tradesmen and craftsmen. They, and the quite different types of economic activity practised by their inhabitants, foreshadowed the future of the town.

Medieval market town

By the thirteenth century Manchester appears in the record as an urban settlement but it was not a politically significant town. The most prominent places in medieval Lancashire were the royal boroughs of Preston, Lancaster, Liverpool and Wigan. These towns enjoyed a much higher status than Manchester, and had comparative autonomy, and wider privileges and liberties. In due course they acquired the full panoply of civic dignity, with mayors, aldermen, corporations, regalia, and a flourishing ceremonial life. Manchester, by comparison, was not to enjoy independent status, with municipal and parliamentary representation, until the nineteenth century (apart from a very brief period in the 1650s during Oliver Cromwell's republic). Nonetheless, the town was developing as an important ecclesiastical and administrative centre. It was the core of a large and wealthy parish and the seat of a great manor, which in turn was the centre of a regionally important barony with landholdings across southern Lancashire.

Parish of Manchester with townships At the time of the Norman Conquest Manchester already had a church. We know from later evidence that its parish was extensive. In the medieval period it covered about sixty square miles, and embraced over two dozen separate townships. (Image drawn by Ian Reid, based on an index map in *Victoria History of the County of Lancashire*, Vol. IV, 1911)

The absence of borough status is an impediment to the historian seeking documentary evidence for the history of the town during these centuries. The lack of a formal council or corporation means a corresponding absence of the historical records (such as burgess rolls) available for more fortunate towns. Additionally, the survival of manorial documents is patchy and often only available for the later period. For example, the series of surviving court leet records, which are of major importance, does not begin until 1552. However, title deeds and other documentary sources have been used to identify the emergence and growth of the town between the post-conquest Norman period and sixteenth and seventeenth centuries.[5]

The medieval town grew up beside the twin focal points of the manor house and the parish church of St Mary. The strategic importance of the site on which the castle and later the manor house were built is no longer apparent, now that the street level is higher and the river Irk is culverted, but they stood on a rocky promontory about forty feet above the confluence of the rivers. The digging of defensive ditches between the rivers enhanced the security of the setting. These ditches roughly followed the modern street

Charter granted to the Burgesses of Manchester 14 May 1301 Medieval Manchester was not legally recognised as a self-governing borough and remained under manorial jurisdiction. However, lord of the manor, Thomas Gresle, granted the burgesses a charter confirming rights and customs. Written in Latin, the Charter of 1301 established a system of local government for the town that, with changes, lasted until the nineteenth century. (Image © Manchester Libraries, Information and Archives)

Hanging Bridge The most important of the town's medieval defences was Hanging Ditch. Hanging Bridge crossed this ditch. By the late seventeenth century Hanging Ditch itself was built over and the bridge lost to view. Remains of the medieval bridge were rediscovered during building work in the late nineteenth century, when this photograph was taken. Today, the bridge is largely hidden by modern buildings, but some of its arches can be seen in the basement of Manchester Cathedral Visitor Centre.
(Image source: Stuart Hylton, *A History of Manchester*, via Wikimedia Commons)

line of Cateaton Street, the northern edge of Exchange Square, Corporation Street, Todd Street and Victoria Station approach. The most important of these defences was Hanging Ditch (commemorated in the modern street name), probably the extension of a natural watercourse, about ten metres wide and over five metres deep in places with a stream flowing through. An imposing stone bridge, Hanging Bridge, crossed this ditch. Dating from the first half of the fourteenth century or earlier, by the sixteenth century huge quantities of rubbish and waste had been tipped into the ravine, and by the late seventeenth century Hanging Ditch itself was built over. In the 1880s, during building work, the medieval bridge was rediscovered and carefully restored. Today, its arches can be viewed in the basement of the Cathedral Visitor Centre.

At one end of the town was Long Millgate, the main access from the north, following the line of the river Irk and at the other the Market Sted (Market Place, long since built over) from which developed Market Sted Lane (Market Street), and finally Deansgate, the route to Chester and the south.

College of Priests (now Chetham's School of Music and Chetham's Library) In 1421 Henry V granted lord of the manor of Manchester, Thomas de la Warre, a licence making the parish church of St Mary's collegiate. To accommodate the new college, de la Warre gave the site of the old fortified manor house on which a range of new buildings were erected using purple-red sandstone obtained from quarries at Collyhurst. The college housed a warden, eight priests or fellows, four clerks and six lay choristers. Today these buildings are the finest of their type and date in the country and a remarkable survival in the heart of the modern city. The college was dissolved by Henry VIII in 1547, but then re-founded and in 1653 acquired by Humphrey Chetham and converted into a residential school (Chetham's Hospital) and free public library (Chetham's Library). With its baronial hall, warden's lodgings (now the library reading room), cloisters and gatehouse, Chetham's is one of Manchester's greatest treasures and of national importance. Above can be seen the warden's lodgings and the porch leading to the baronial hall and below is the west cloister walkway. (Image above courtesy of terry6082 Books, and below, Pew Pew Pew! Lasers! via Wikimedia Commons)

At an early date a bridge was built across the Irwell linking Manchester and Salford. Originally in timber, this was rebuilt in stone in 1325. In common with most medieval towns, and especially those that had market and borough charters, Manchester developed a pattern of burgage plots, which were either leased directly from the lord or held by burgage tenure. Burgages were long, narrow plots of land stretching back at right angles from a narrow street frontage. Holders of burgage plots were tenants who paid a small annual rent to the lord of the manor, but over time the rental income for the lord became negligible and burgage plots effectively became freeholds. This form of land tenure is significant, because it contrasted with the more restrictive forms of feudal tenure that were widespread in the countryside, and it gave the opportunity for burgage holders to develop commercial and entrepreneurial activities, including the accumulation of land to form property portfolios. Burgage tenure attracted incomers who, in addition to houses, might construct workshops on the long plot behind the street. These open spaces, such as yards and gardens, slowly disappeared as buildings were crammed into them, and after the medieval period they were prime building land because plots in the central area came at a premium.

Urban growth up to the early fourteenth century was confined to the immediate vicinity of the manor house and parish church. After this the town expanded north as Long Millgate was developed, and east, with evidence of growth along Market Sted Lane by 1417. However, urban growth was slow and the town's character was still markedly rural. As late as 1500 Market Sted Lane comprised little more than an assortment of barns and closes with a few houses, and the eastern side of Long Millgate was lined with orchards. It was along these two thoroughfares that most new houses were to be built as the town grew during the sixteenth century. A striking feature of land ownership in later medieval Manchester was the role of the Church. Ecclesiastical ownership of urban land was common to all medieval towns, but the proportion was particularly high in Manchester and, after the lord of the manor, the Church was the major landholder. This was mainly due to the growth of chantry lands in the later medieval period, whereby the rent income from property was allocated to support chapels where masses were chanted for the souls of the dead. For example, the Church acquired much of the land between Deansgate and the Irwell (Parsonage). However, the Church did not act as a barrier to economic growth or urban variety. Indeed it actively encouraged building on its holdings in Long Millgate and Market Sted Lane, so much so that by the sixteenth century nearly half the houses in the town were subject to ecclesiastical rents.

The pace of such acquisitions was accelerated when, in 1421, the parish church of St Mary's was made collegiate: that is, a royal licence was obtained from Henry V, which created a college of priests to serve in the church, headed by a warden. This is one of the first signs that the town was slowly moving up the ranks to assume a greater importance, because associated with it was the rebuilding of the parish church. The Norman church of St Mary was, by Lancashire's modest standards, comparatively large, though only fragmentary evidence of it survives. It was probably rebuilt piecemeal in the thirteenth century, but was presumably nothing very remarkable. But in 1421 came a dramatic change. Thomas de la Warre was not only rector of Manchester, but was also the lord of the manor. His lasting impact on the town was his project to rebuild the parish church and securing the licence to make it collegiate. To accommodate the new college he granted it the site and buildings of the old fortified manor house. These were rebuilt to create what was then known as Christ's College and later as Chetham's College, the finest buildings of their type and date in the country and a truly miraculous survivor in the heart of the modern city. The college was dissolved by Henry VIII in 1547, but then re-founded and in 1653 was acquired by Humphrey Chetham and converted into a residential school (Chetham's Hospital) and free public library (Chetham's Library). With its baronial hall, great chamber (now the library reading room), cloister courtyard and gatehouse, Chetham's is one of Manchester's greatest treasures and of national importance.

Meanwhile, the parish church itself was being rebuilt in spectacular style. The new building, constructed between the mid-1420s and about 1510, is today (despite its extensive restoration by the Victorians) one of the most impressive examples in England of a late medieval collegiate church. It was immensely wide, partly because of the eight separate chantry chapels which by the 1520s occupied its side aisles. The nave has a magnificent decorated wooden roof with carved minstrel angels as ornamental supports (each playing a different instrument), and the choir stalls and misericords are among the finest in the north of England, similar in style to those in Ripon Minster and Beverley Minster. All of this betokened a perceptible change in Manchester's fortunes. By the early sixteenth century the quiet market town was dominated by an architectural showpiece emblematic of the wealth of the parish as well as the rising fortunes and the regional prominence of the town.

But although the town grew gradually in importance as well as size, it could not escape the clutches of the lord of the manor. Whereas in the sixteenth and seventeenth centuries towns such as Liverpool and Wigan, already royal boroughs, were granted charters of incorporation, which made

Collegiate Church (now Manchester Cathedral) The former parish church was rebuilt when it was made collegiate in the fifteenth century. It became the Cathedral of the newly created Diocese of Manchester in 1847. This image, first published in 1829, shows the collegiate church before it was extensively restored in the nineteenth and twentieth centuries. (Image © Alamy)

them fully self-governing, Manchester remained as a seigneurial borough with more limited freedoms. The town did enjoy some basic privileges. The right to an annual fair was obtained in 1223, and by 1282 the townsmen were free from compulsory labour on the lord's lands. However, they still owed their lord various feudal forms of fealty such as heriot, a duty or tribute due to a lord on the death of a tenant, perhaps an echo of the military character of the *buhr* in the days of the Danish kings. By later medieval times such dues were frequently converted to cash payments.[6] The burgesses did have the right to hold their own court, the portmoot, distinct from the baron's court and with wider powers than the hallmoots held in the sub-manors. In 1301 Thomas Gresle granted a charter confirming the existing customs and privileges enjoyed by the townsmen. Here, as in many other towns the granting of a charter simply allowed the manorial lord to take control of a market that was already flourishing. The market long predated any formal recognition, and in Manchester's case no formal charter granting market rights was issued.

The market was 'customary' – that is, it had arisen informally and was held according to long-established tradition.

This charter of 1301 was nonetheless a landmark in the history of the town. It established the system of local government for Manchester that was to survive for over five centuries. Among its clauses was one granting the burgesses the right to 'elect anyone they please from among themselves to be reeve, and to remove the reeve'. Although not a mayor as would have been the case in a legally recognised borough, the boroughreeve (as he was confusingly to be called) had some important and comparable duties. But his role had inherent contradictions, for he was both the representative of the burgesses in their dealings with the lord of the manor and also responsible to the lord for the maintenance of order and the observance of regulations. He was to collect all burgage rents, levy market tolls, and apprehend offenders and secure their appearance at court to stand trial. After 1301 as a manorial borough, Manchester had a legal status it shared with many other important places (for example, Bolton, Birmingham, Sheffield, Bradford, and its nearest neighbour, Salford). Although it grew ever more important economically and commercially, far outstripping its regional neighbours, Manchester was not given incorporation.

Why did Manchester remain unincorporated? Manchester's administrative status was a matter of legal definition. The possession of burgage tenure and a portmoot had given recognition as a 'free borough' in earlier days, but by the fourteenth century the term *liber burgus* had taken on a narrower and more technical meaning. It was judicially determined in 1359 that the charter of 1301 had not granted borough status and that Manchester should be regarded as a *villae mercatoriae*, a market town, and not a borough.[7] This judgment represented a successful attempt by the manorial lord to prevent the town achieving self-government. Exactly similar challenges to borough status were taking place elsewhere at this time – for example, at nearby Warrington. As a *seigneurial borough* Manchester was a town of local importance only in what was in the Middle Ages one of the most economically backward and sparsely populated parts of the country. That being said, it may be reasonable to assume that the town's wealth grew steadily. The annual fair, traditionally held over two days on Acres Field, arable land adjacent to the town, part of which space now forms St Ann's Square, was the first to be founded in the Salford Hundred and only the fourth in south Lancashire. This and the customary Saturday market signify the town's trading function.

Industry

Given its later economic progress, one key question is whether or not there is evidence of industry in medieval Manchester. In the fourteenth century the manufacture of woollen cloth was the principal industry in England, and the export of wool from British flocks was by far the country's most important international trade. Wool was sufficiently important for Edward III to order that the Lord Chancellor should sit on a woolsack as a reminder of the importance of the trade to the nation. In tracing the early origins and distribution of commercial textile production (as contrasted with purely domestic output) the presence of a water-powered fulling mill is often taken as reliable evidence. Fulling is the process whereby woollen cloth was finished by being beaten to felt the fibres and to rid it of grease and dirt. This process could be undertaken with greater speed and economy in a fulling mill than when the processing was done by hand or foot, but this was only viable on a relatively large scale, so a mill is seen as indicative of a commercial undertaking. There were several such mills in north-west England by the thirteenth century, including one on the river Irk in Manchester, dated by historians to as early as 1282.[8] According to one theory, nearby Hanging Ditch may have been named because fullers hung their cloth out to drain and dry over this watercourse.

The development of fulling mills, exploiting abundant local waterpower, caused a shift in cloth production from the lowland towns of eastern England (such as York, Lincoln, Stamford, Northampton and Colchester) which had dominated the early medieval cloth trade to more rural locations on the swift, clear streams of the north of England and the West Country. However, in the thirteenth and fourteenth centuries such mills were much more numerous in north Lancashire, around Lancaster and into the Lake District, than in the Manchester area.[9] South-east Lancashire was not yet a major centre for cloth production.

The main rival to the English trade was the Flemish woollen industry, based on the centres of Ghent, Bruges and Ypres, which was enjoying a period of expansion. English monarchs tried repeatedly to deal with the competition from Flanders by restricting exports of English wool to the Flemish workshops and by enticing skilled Flemish wool workers to emigrate to England. During the fourteenth century economic and social unrest in Flanders did indeed result in significant migration, and communities of incomers became settled in, among other places, London, Norwich and, apparently, Manchester, bringing with them new skills and techniques. The exact number of Flemish migrant weavers is not known, but their presence is reflected in the improved quality of the English cloth, which gradually

Cathedral Nave The function of the college of priests was to chant masses for the souls of the dead. To this end chantry chapels were constructed along the north and south sides of the church on either side of the nave. Chantries were abolished during the Reformation. The defining screens were later removed making it look like double aisles on each side of the nave, which is consequently much wider than it is long. (Photograph by Mike Peel)

Angels in the nave roof The Cathedral nave roof brackets are supported by fourteen angel sculptures, each playing a different late medieval instrument; the south side has stringed instruments, and the north side mostly wind instruments. These are dated to the rebuilding of the collegiate nave and choir in the late fifteenth century. (Images © Carnegie Publishing)

Misericords Misericords are the seats of the choir stalls, which when tipped allow a person to rest on the bracket or ledge giving the appearance of standing. The name comes from the Latin word for pity, 'misericordia', out of pity for weary priests during long services. They were common in medieval churches. Often the undersides of the seats were carved and, since they would be rarely seen, gave scope to the carpenter to depict scenes from everyday life and legend that were rarely religious. These carvings offer a revealing insight into the medieval mind. Many were destroyed or damaged in the ensuing centuries. There are 30 stalls in the choir of Manchester Cathedral and all the misericords survive. They date from the early sixteenth century and are among the finest in the country. (Images © Carnegie Publishing)

The Establishment of Flemish Weavers in Manchester A.D. 1363 by Ford Madox Brown, mural in the Great Hall of Manchester Town Hall. (Image in public domain, via Wikimedia Commons)

became an export article whereas exports of raw wool dropped dramatically. Traditionally the arrival of Flemish weavers in Manchester was taken as marking the origins of the textile industry in the town. When the Victorian city fathers sought an ancient lineage for the Manchester trade they included the arrival of the Flemish weavers among the subjects for Ford Madox Brown's famous murals in Manchester Town Hall. In reality, the woollen industry was already established in and around Manchester long before the supposed arrival of the Flemings.

Manchester was not yet a notable centre for craft production, and there is no evidence of the existence of craft guilds of the sort that existed in many boroughs. Nonetheless, we have clear evidence of commercial activity from the late fourteenth century, when Robert, Richard and Thomas Parker traded as 'drapers' between 1380 and 1405. We know something of the breadth of their trading connections because they had debts in Furness, Lancaster and as far away as Coventry. There are also indications that other specialist craftsmen were working in Manchester, including knife-makers, shoemakers and even possibly a goldsmith. Excavations in the vicinity of Hanging Ditch, immediately south of the cathedral, have revealed quantities of trade waste from the late medieval period, including over 200 pieces of leather (offcuts and leather objects such as shoes).[10] These are indications that the town was growing in wealth and that its traders were starting to develop commercial links outside the immediate area. But we must not overstate the case. Manchester was not a significant trading or craft centre such as the medieval woollen towns of Leicester, Coventry, Exeter and Norwich.

The town must be placed in its regional context. Analysis of the limited evidence about the economy of north-west England in the later Middle Ages gives a picture of relative weakness, with Lancashire consistently registering as the poorest county in the land. An assessment of lay and clerical wealth finds no improvement in Lancashire's position over the 200 years from 1334 to 1535. Much of the county was thinly populated and although a per capita estimate of wealth might have placed it higher, it is the absence of significant improvement over a long time period that is perhaps most striking.[11] Since such financial assessments are based on data for the county of Lancaster as a whole they may hide the comparatively better performance of Manchester parish. Indirect evidence would suggest so. The mere fact that the rebuilding of the parish church was to such a grand scale is an indication of advancing prosperity and in itself would add to the town's prestige. However, in the absence of direct evidence we cannot say whether, as seems quite probable, the roots of later economic success were laid down during the fourteenth and fifteenth centuries or were instead the achievement of the Tudor period alone.

Burgage plots in Manchester 1301–1800 In common with most medieval towns, and especially those that had market or borough charters, Manchester developed a pattern of burgage plots, which were either leased directly from the lord or held by burgage tenure. Burgages were long, narrow plots of land stretching back at right angles from a narrow street frontage. Over time burgage plots effectively became freeholds allowing burgage holders to develop commercial and entrepreneurial activities. (Image from Michael Morris, *Medieval Manchester*, Greater Manchester Archaeological Unit, 1983, p. 36, courtesy of Greater Manchester Archaeological Advisory Service Archive)

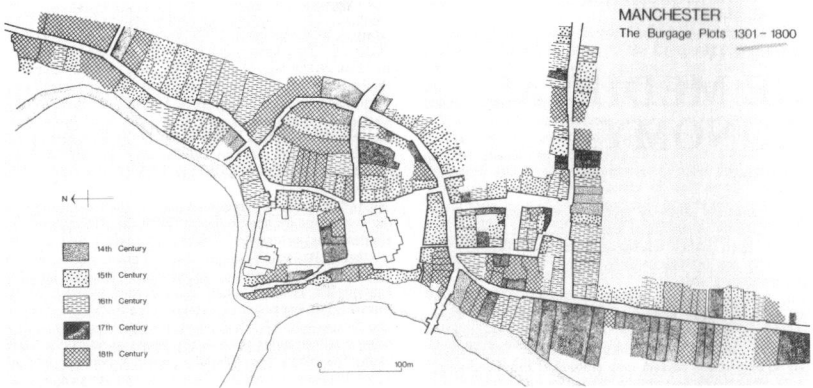

Mamecestre: a medieval market town

3

'The faireſt, beſt builded, quikkeſt and moſt populous tounne of al Lancaſtreshire': Mancheſter 1543–1660

DURING the sixteenth and seventeenth centuries Manchester grew in population size and economic significance. It was transformed from the small country market town of the medieval period into the emerging provincial capital of north-west England. By 1660 it was second only to Chester as the leading town of the region, and its national importance and influence were growing fast. Like other provincial towns, such as Birmingham, Leeds and Hull, Manchester shared in the dynamism that increasingly characterised the English economy. During this period the centre of gravity of the European economy shifted decisively from the Mediterranean to the lands bordering the North Sea and the English Channel, as Holland and England became the dominant commercial powers. Manchester prospered greatly as a result of this change. During the Tudor and Stuart periods, long before the industrial revolution, and many decades before the steam-powered mechanisation of cotton production, Manchester had already earned a reputation as a specialist cloth town which combined manufacture with trade. This is an important point, for in the popular mythology Manchester was a mushroom-like product of the industrial revolution in the late eighteenth century. That perception is entirely inaccurate: not only was it a market town before 1500, but it was also a significant commercial and manufacturing centre by 1700, several generations before the town's first steam-powered cotton mill began production.

Prosperous places grow in size, and evidence of progress can be found in the available population data. Until the middle of the sixteenth century we have no way of estimating Manchester's population, and not until 1801 was there a national census. Historians have to base their calculations on data collected by contemporaries for quite different purposes. These sources are of variable completeness, and none is ideal, but nonetheless general patterns and trends may be inferred. Deductions drawn from the lay subsidy returns of 1543 suggest that in the mid-sixteenth century the population of the township of Manchester consisted of about 2,000 souls. This does not make Tudor Manchester of national importance. Across England at this time there were perhaps fifteen provincial towns with populations in excess of 5,000 and many more with 3,000–4,000 inhabitants. Within the relatively un-urbanised North West, however, the town was certainly one of the more important centres.

Manchester's population seems to have risen slowly in the second half of the sixteenth century, with fluctuations due to epidemic disease and other mortality factors such as bad harvests. In the early seventeenth century growth appears to have accelerated, and some calculations have suggested that by the 1640s the town had almost 4,000 inhabitants. However, this was to be a truly devastating decade when perhaps one-third of the town's population died in an outbreak of plague that occurred in 1645, a catastrophe which itself followed the ravages and disruption of the Civil War. It is a measure of the economic dynamism of Manchester at this time that population levels seem to have recovered by the 1660s. The hearth tax returns for 1664 suggest that Manchester and Salford together had over 5,000 inhabitants. This may be compared with, for example, population figures of 2,750 for Macclesfield, 1,900 in Preston, 1,670 in Bolton, 1,450 in Stockport, and only 1,350 in Liverpool.[1] These figures are inevitably speculative but even if only approximately reliable they suggest a town whose population had more than doubled in a century, a rate of growth that surpassed the national average of 68 per cent between 1563 and 1664 and the average for Lancashire and Cheshire of 64 per cent over the same period.[2]

As well as showing evidence of a rising population, by the sixteenth century Manchester appears much more frequently in the historical record. Because of the greater range and quantity of reliable documentary sources we can discover much more about the character and life of the town and its people. For example, the surviving records of the court leet begin in 1552 and continue in a broken run through to the purchase of the manorial rights by the new municipal authority in 1846 (1687–1731 are missing). From being seriously under-documented, Manchester becomes one of the better-recorded towns of Elizabethan England, and from this exceptional source we gain remarkable insights into people's occupations and trade as well as how Manchester was managed and governed. Historians have also made good use of wills and inventories as sources for the economic and social life of the town. There are few surviving pre-Reformation wills, but from the 1540s they became much more numerous and, crucially, provide much evidence about the merchants, traders and craftsmen whose activities were generating the economic dynamism of sixteenth- and seventeenth-century Manchester.

These sources, together with other local documents and the state papers for the era, give us a much clearer picture of the town during the reigns of the Tudor and Stuart monarchs than for its history under their medieval predecessors. Moreover, we have our first eyewitness descriptions of the place, provided by contemporary visitors such as John Leland, the King's Antiquary. His assessment of Manchester when he visited in the 1540s appears in the title to this chapter. The overall impression given by these sources is of a town which, though still politically of little importance, had assumed the economic leadership of its region. What kind of place was it? These are Leland's words:

> Mancestre on the south side of Irwel River stondith in Salfordshire, and is the fairest, best builded, quikkest, and most populous tounne in al Lancastreshire; yet is in hit but one paroch chirch, but is a college. ... Ther be divers stone bridgis in the toune, but the best of iii [3] arches is over Irwel, cawllid Salford Bridge. This bridge devideth Manchestre from Salford, the wich is as a large suburbe to Manchestre. On this bridge is a praty little chapel. The next is the bridge that is over Hirke river, on the wich the fair builded college standith as in the veri point of the mouth of hit. ... On Hirk [Irk] river be divers fair milles that serve the toune. In the towne be ii [2] fair market placys. And almost ii flyte shottes withowt the towne beneth on the same side of Irwel yet be seene the dikes and fundations of Old Man Castel yn a ground now enclosed. The stones of the ruines of this castel wer translatid toward making of bridgges for the tounne. [*The Itinerary of John Leland in or about the years 1535-1543* Ed. Lucy Toulmin Smith, vol.4, George Bell & Sons, 1909]

At this time the built-up area of the town of Manchester was little larger than during the medieval centuries. The church, the college, and the market place clustered together in a compact huddle on land raised high above the confluence of the Irwell and the Irk. Hanging Ditch, which had separated church from market place, was already largely filled in with refuse. To this medieval core had been added the grammar school, which was founded in

John Dee (1527–1608) Mathematician and astrologer, advisor to Queen Elizabeth, and warden of Christ's College, Manchester between 1595 and 1608. Portrait in the collection of the Ashmolean Museum by an unknown artist at about the time Dee assumed the wardenship in Manchester. (Image in public domain, via Wikimedia Commons)

1515 by Hugh Oldham, the Manchester-born bishop of Exeter and occupied the gatehouse of the college. The ancient thoroughfares of Deansgate and Millgate were still the main entry points from south and north respectively. Manorial rentals show that houses and shops lined these as they approached the town centre. Market Sted Lane was starting to acquire its later significance as the commercial focus of the town, and was also the location of the conduit from which Tudor Manchester drew most of its fresh water.

However, despite population growth and new building, the town remained small and the townspeople were never far from the countryside. To the east were fields and woods, including Wythengreave or Withy Grove, 'the small wood of willows'. Farmland still reached down to the Irwell and agriculture continued to play an important part in the local economy. This was the town that the antiquarian and topographer William Camden visited in 1585, forty years after John Leland. Manchester later appears in his monumental work of geography and history, *Britannia*:

> But where Irke and Irwell meet together, on the left bank, raised of a reddish kind of ston, scarce three miles from Mersey, flourished that town of right great antiquity which we now call Manchester, and Antonine the Emperour called Mancunum and Manucium, according to the variety of the Copies. This, retaining the first part of his ancient name, farre excelleth the townes lying round about it for the beautifull shew it carieth, for resort unto it, and for clothing, in regard also of the mercate place, the faire Church, and Colledge founded by Thomas Lord De-la-ware. … But in the foregoing age this towne was of farre greater account both for certain wollen clothes there wrought and in great request, commonly called Manchester Cottons. [William Camden, *Britannia*, 1607, English translation by Philomen Holland, 1610.]

'Manchester cottons'

As in most towns of this period, there was in Manchester a wide variety of employment opportunities, but by the middle of the sixteenth century it is quite clear that the manufacture and sale of cloth predominated. As Camden notes, Manchester surpassed the neighbouring towns in the production of the woollen cloths known, very confusingly to later generations, as 'Manchester cottons'. These had nothing to do with the cotton fibre later so famously linked with the town: rather, Manchester cottons were a variety of woollen cloth, possibly so called because of the 'cottoning', or raising of the nap, that was part of the cloth manufacturing process. Four main types of woollen cloth were being manufactured in Lancashire at this time: rugs, friezes, kerseys and cottons. Rugs and friezes were the coarser and heavier weaves, kerseys and cottons the lighter. The production of kerseys was concentrated in the north and east of the county while cottons were produced in Manchester and the surrounding area as well around Kendal, further north in Westmorland.[3] However, the Lancashire textile trade had two distinct components in the years around 1600: the making of woollen cloth and the weaving of linens. In Manchester the linen industry rivalled woollen manufacture, using yarn (produced from flax) mostly imported from Ireland, with a small quantity from Lancashire. The woollen and linen cloths manufactured in and around Manchester were sold throughout the provinces as well as on the London cloth market, which had a separate section named the 'Manchester Hall'. It is significant and revealing that Manchester's identity was already associated with trade and that the town had given its name to a particular type of cloth.

Although the woollen and linen trades advanced the wealth of Manchester clothiers, attracted migrant workers, and identified the town on the London markets, it did not mean that the town was yet of national importance. The diversity of Manchester's economy may have made it the most prosperous place in sixteenth-century Lancashire, but the county itself remained, as it had been in the late medieval period, among the poorest and most isolated in the land. This is the historical consensus. But the degree of isolation should not be exaggerated. Manchester and some other Lancashire towns were forging national and international connections through trade. For example, as early as the 1540s the Bristol merchant, John Smythe, was getting Manchester cottons from Thomas Abeck of Manchester in return for wine, wool, oil, and woad. The cottons were for export to Spain and Portugal. Smythe also sold iron and wine to James Webster of Manchester.[4] Such trading links were to blossom and flourish over the next hundred years. Moreover, by the early sixteenth century changes had occurred in the relative distribution of wealth within Lancashire itself. In the early fourteenth century arable farming and close proximity to Chester had made the south-west of the county the most prosperous, and the area around Manchester was poor by comparison, but by 1525 the south-east of the county was the most affluent.[5] It seems certain that this change had come about largely because of the rise of the textile industry.

We do not know exactly when its economic rise to pre-eminence began but, as we have seen, there is clear evidence that contemporaries regarded Manchester as the most important cloth town in Lancashire, wealthier than places such as Bolton, Bury or Preston which were also visited by Leland. We also know something of the organisation of cloth manufacturing and trading in the sixteenth century. At this time most production – though not all – was carried out by independent weavers working in their own homes. Weaving was therefore domestic in setting and normally functioned in very small units. The weavers bought their own raw materials (primarily the yarn) and sold their finished cloth direct to merchant clothiers. There was little evidence as yet of the 'putting-out' system that came to characterise the Lancashire cloth industry by the late seventeenth century. This was the practice whereby capitalist clothiers controlled the trade directly, distributing the raw materials to dependent cottage workers and paying them by the piece.

However, the independence of the weavers in the early modern period must not be overstated. Although they were not subject to piece rates like their eighteenth-century descendants (which meant, in effect, wage dependency) they often relied heavily upon credit extended by the clothier and they were in some senses 'employed' by country 'manufacturers' who acted as middlemen between them and the urban merchants.

These urban merchants, the Manchester clothiers, were the key figures in the production process. Most of them, mainly men but also including a few women such as widows who had inherited property and stock, were themselves also involved directly in production. They were not solely merchants, for after they had bought the cloth from the weavers they undertook the shearing and sometimes the dyeing themselves, eventually selling the final product, often on the London market. Thus the homes of these men also functioned as workshops and warehouses. An interesting example from Elizabeth's reign is George Holt of Salford, who died in 1572. The inventory of his possessions at his death included a 'workehowse' with carding equipment, three spinning wheels, three looms, a shear-board and several pairs of shears. This implies that all the processes of cloth manufacture, except fulling, were carried out there. Holt may have had up to fifteen people working under one roof and although some must have been members of his own family it is likely that he was also an employer of labour. He ran a thriving business, with almost 150 stones of wool (nearly a ton) in a chamber of the house and large amounts of finished cloth stored in a 'ware howse'. Moreover, the list of debts owing to him indicates that he had also sold substantial amounts of cloth. However, even such a large-scale producer as Holt combined agriculture with manufacture. He farmed an acre of oats, half an acre of barley, had two ploughs, four cows and a horse, and also kept bees in his back garden.[6]

Manchester merchants

By the early seventeenth century the woollen trade in Manchester had come to be dominated by a small group of wealthy clothiers, several of whom were connected by marriage. Chief among them were members of the Mosley family, who emerged as prominent cloth dealers in Elizabeth's reign and made a speciality of buying local cloth for sale in the London market. When Anthony Mosley died in 1607 he left a personal estate of over £2,000. His brother Nicholas rose to prominence in London, becoming lord mayor, and was knighted by Elizabeth, partly for his role in raising the finance to help fight the Spanish Armada in 1588. Nicholas bought the manor of Manchester in 1596 and appears to have been assiduous in the pursuit of his rights as lord. When Anthony died his sons, Oswald and Francis, inherited his property. The Mosleys were linked by marriage to the Tipping family and formed part of an intricate network of familial and business relations that connected the wealthy Manchester clothiers. George Tipping's former apprentice, George Chetham, became his partner in 1610 and the Chetham family as a whole soon rose to unparalleled prominence in the town. Among other members of this elite group were Thomas Lancashire, Thomas Heape and Francis Locker. They seem to have functioned primarily as merchant manufacturers, concerned with the finishing and marketing of woollen cloth, although some may also have dealt in linens and fustians. This coterie of the wealthiest merchants was not entirely typical: most clothiers, like George Holt, still combined farming with manufacturing. Nevertheless, the rise of a mercantile elite has been taken as evidence of the economic freedom engendered by the absence of guilds in the town and the consequent lack of restrictions on the entry of newcomers into trades (although, it is possible that the effects of the 1605 outbreak of plague may have exaggerated the concentration of the woollen industry in such a few hands).[7]

The emergence of a network of wealthy merchants by the early seventeenth century was a clear indicator of the growing importance of the town's trade. Even more significantly, this followed the point in the later sixteenth century when Lancashire cloth producers first began to diversify and to introduce new fabrics. Most significantly, cotton fibre was first introduced to the region through the manufacture of fustian cloth, a hard-wearing mixture of linen yarn with cotton. This, with the introduction of the 'new draperies' (imitations of the lighter Italian worsteds) and the diversification of linen production into smallwares such as tapes, garters, and ribbons, has led some historians to refer to the period around 1600 as a 'minor industrial revolution'.[8] Fustian production spread rapidly throughout south-east Lancashire, into the Bolton, Blackburn and Oldham areas as well as the villages of the parish of Manchester. Fustians had the advantage of not being subject to the aulnage, a system whereby woollen cloth was taxed once it was ready for sale. The development of fustian production strengthened even further the hold of the wealthy Manchester clothiers on the textile trade of the region. Since fustians required cotton wool, imports of which were controlled by a monopoly held by the Levant Company in London, weavers were dependent for supplies of this essential

Humphrey Chetham (1580–1653) It is because of a charitable bequest in his will that today Humphrey Chetham is one of the best-known names from Manchester's past. He left money to purchase land of sufficient value to endow forty places for poor boys from Manchester and for a building to accommodate them and further money for the provision of a free public library for Manchester. Chetham had long wanted to use the college buildings, and in 1654 the feoffees of his new charities were able to buy them and in the following year Chetham's Hospital and Library were opened. This is the only known portrait of the wealthy merchant and financier and today it hangs in the reading room of Chetham's Library. (Image in public domain, via Wikimedia Commons)

new raw material upon the wealthy clothiers who alone had the capital to underwrite the trade and who could afford to maintain a resident factor in London or other ports. Fustian prices tended to be relatively stable, and remained high throughout the seventeenth century, so the incentive of a good profit was always there for those with sufficient capital. By the 1620s

Chetham's Library book shelves The library west range with shelves and stools dating from the 1650s. (Photograph by Mike Peel)

Chetham's Library Reading Room This was originally part of the warden's lodgings. (Photograph by Michael D. Beckwith, via Wikimedia Commons)

there were three leading fustian trading partnerships in Manchester, each a family concern: Henry and Joshua Wrigley, Humphrey and Robert Booth, and George and Humphrey Chetham.

Such successful partnerships were rooted in local family and business connections stretching back a century and more. The best documented are the Chetham brothers.[9] Descended from yeoman farming stock, by the mid-sixteenth century, we know that they were selling woollens to merchants in Hull, Chester and Liverpool, and dealing in flax and yarn in south-east Lancashire. This local activity enabled them to build up a crucial network of market relationships, in which trust and credit worthiness were essential, though they also retained an interest in land and accumulated a sizeable property portfolio. In his will of 1571 James Chetham (grandfather of Humphrey) detailed 'landes, tenements, trackes and burgagees lyeing in Kersall, Manchester and Cromsall or els wheresoever they be'. Through steady accumulation of capital he had built up his landholdings simultaneously with developing the cloth business. To his son Henry he bequeathed 163 acres in Kersal in addition to messuages and burgages in Manchester and Ashton-under-Lyne. James, Henry's eldest son, carried on the wool dealing, while his younger brothers, Humphrey and George, were apprenticed to Manchester drapers. They later pooled their resources (including annuities from their father as well as other legacies and assets derived from family connections) to become partners in trade themselves. Humphrey and George began trading in the new fustians in 1614, with George based in London and Humphrey in Manchester. They sold raw wool, flax, and cotton fibre to spinners, and yarns to weavers, then bought the finished yarn or cloth and sold it on the London market. When the partnership was renewed in 1619 it was valued at about £10,000. The surplus profits were invested in land purchases, chief of which was the 340-acre country estate of Clayton Hall, north-east of Manchester on the road to Ashton-under-Lyne. After George died in 1627, Humphrey acquired further property, notably the lordship of Turton near Bolton, including Turton Tower, a medieval fortified house. By 1640 he had become one of the largest landowners in the region, as well as its greatest merchant.

The other outlet for his growing cash surplus was money-lending. From the early 1620s onwards he became a financier on a substantial scale, at first lending to his numerous relatives and later to the gentry and merchants of south Lancashire and north Cheshire. The scale of the lending was such that by 1640 he was operating *de facto* a sizeable banking house. Like many of his era Chetham also sought to spend surplus cash on philanthropic ventures, and it is because of a charitable bequest in his will that today his is one of the best-known names from Manchester's past. In his lifetime he had provided for the maintenance and education of 14 poor boys and attempted unsuccessfully to obtain the buildings of Manchester College which were, in his words, 'spoyld and ruin'd and become like a dunghill', as a hospital for them. What he could not achieve in his lifetime was secured by money left in his will, which allocated £7,500 to the purchase of land of sufficient value to endow forty places for poor boys from Manchester and for a building to accommodate them. He also left over £1,000 to be spent on the provision of a free public library in Manchester. Chetham had long wanted to use the college buildings, and in 1654 the feoffees of his new charities were able to buy them. In December 1656 the Chetham's Hospital and Library were opened.

Early town government: the court leet

The wealthier inhabitants of the town were expected to take part in its public life. Humphrey Chetham served as a juror in 1619 but later, because of his eminence and financial resources, assumed office at county level (he was high sheriff for Lancashire in 1634–35). Others took part in the various activities of the court leet of the manor of Manchester, which in the sixteenth century evolved from the baronial court and portmoot of the medieval period – although the legal status of the court has bemused historians as much as it apparently confused contemporaries. In Tudor times its proceedings reflected almost every aspect of the town's life and 'all and every the inhabitants and householders of the town of Manchester' were summoned to attend the half-yearly meetings, at Easter and at Michaelmas. These were presided over by the lord's steward (who was often a local lawyer), while the lord's clerk recorded the proceedings. When the steward summoned the townspeople to attend he named at least twelve burgesses to act as jurors. These men were drawn from the leading families of the town and the same names appear repeatedly in the jury lists. The court remained manorial in principle, claiming jurisdiction over the whole barony, and in its structure resembling the courts of small rural manors. However, by 1600 it was already, in effect, a form of town government: its jurors were all burgesses of the town, and most of the business transacted was town's business.

The first duty of jurors at the Michaelmas court leet was to elect the officers of the town for the ensuing year, most of whom were unpaid. First in eminence was the boroughreeve, the man who, in the absence of a mayor, served as the leading townsman. Much of the difficult work was undertaken by his assistants, including the 'catchpole' or bailiff, a paid and salaried officer who collected fines and carried out distraints in cases of 'divers trespasses and offences'. An efficient catchpole might remain in post for several years. In practical terms, the most important of the elected unpaid officials were the constables of Manchester with their powers to arrest felons and persons 'making Riots, Debates, or Frays, or breaking the Peace'. They also held responsibility for raising the 'hue-and-cry' against horse-stealers and housebreakers, and for enforcing the statutes against vagrancy and begging. They had the use of the town 'lock-up' or 'Dungeon', a small former chapel on Salford Bridge across the Irwell. The constables had the right to call on any townsman to serve as a 'watchman' to protect Manchester by day or night, although as the town grew this before long evolved into the employment of paid watchmen. The constables were also responsible for a myriad financial and executive matters, and it was little wonder that – as they were unpaid – some of those elected to the office proved markedly reluctant to serve.

As well as these chief officers of the town there was a very wide variety of minor officials. Lists of positions and those elected can be found in the court leet records for each year. As early as the 1580s around 60–70 were elected at each Michaelmas meeting – a remarkably large figure for a town of little more than 2,000 people – and by the middle years of the seventeenth century the number had reached 120. It fluctuated around this figure for the next hundred years. The responsibilities of this myriad petty officials varied from ensuring the observance of market regulations to enforcing the responsibility of each householder to cleanse his own street frontage ('scavengers' were elected for every part of town). Paid cleaners were employed to sweep the Marketsted, which inevitably acquired quantities of litter each market day. None of this should suggest that the town was comprehensively policed, but early modern local government depended heavily on the co-operation and involvement of local people. The huge number and variety of unpaid officials should be taken as evidence of this. It spread the weight of responsibility widely and also represented a relatively light hand of authority for those townspeople of substance. However, it meted out harsh treatment to outsiders who had little to contribute to the prosperity of the town.

Manchester was becoming a lively and bustling place with a fluctuating population of comers and goers seeking work and residence or passing through. It was, for example, a common port of call for those travelling to and from Ireland, while its location at the meeting point of national highways from Yorkshire, the Midlands, Derbyshire and the northern counties meant that people from most parts of England had relatively easy access to the town. The lack of guild restrictions had made Manchester a comparatively open place, inviting to newcomers. But the repeated mention, in the court leet records, of the presence of 'forrainers and strangers' suggests considerable anxiety over those newcomers who were unable to support themselves and who might therefore become a charge on the poor rate. Thus, from 1614 the constables were supported by a paid 'Beadle or Marshall … for the better restraining of wandering rogues, vagabonds and sturdy beggars'. His wages were meagre but were supplemented by the payment of four pence for every rogue he whipped.[10] Justice was usually meted out in a public place, and in 1625 a pillory and stocks were erected in the Market Place for the general chastisement of miscreants. Justice could also be retributive. For example, in 1573 it was ordered that

Humphrey Booth the Elder A modern stone plaque at the junction of Oxford Street and Portland Street commemorates the fustian merchant who by a deed of feoffment in 1630 granted to trustees the management of lands worth £20 a year which were then fields at Piccadilly and Oxford Street. The deed stated that the income from these lands should be used for the relief of poor, aged or impotent persons dwelling in the town of Salford, and Booth's Charity, as it became known, made small grants of money and provided clothing and blankets for the poor. Later, his grandson Humphrey Booth the Younger left lands in Salford to provide an income that should also 'be distributed amongst the Poore of Salford … as the Money's left by my Grandfather is'. The Booth Charities still operate today. (Image © Carnegie Publishing)

what person soever shall be founde drunken in any Alehowse within this Towne or els sene abroad in the strets shall therefore be punysshed all night in the Dongeon, And moreover pay presently when they be released vj^d to the Constables to be geaven to the poore And if the saide person be so poore that he cannot paye the same Then the good man or good wife of the howse where he continued Drynkinge shall paie the saide fine.[11]

A key area of responsibility was the policing of the weekly markets. In fact what we know about this central element in the town's life derives chiefly from the attempts of the court leet to regulate it. The markets and the annual fairs were a valuable source of revenue for the lord of the manor, with stallage fees and tolls paid direct to his own official. The main concern of the court leet was to safeguard the food supply and to ensure the wholesome quality of the food sold, an important matter in an era when dearth was commonplace and a wet summer could mean a failed harvest and consequent food shortages and increased prices of essential foodstuffs. Market regulations were strengthened following such scarcities. Regulations require officials to enforce them and fines to be paid for infringements. The court leet appointed a bewildering array of officials from ale tasters and 'officers for holesome bread' to a variety of market-lookers for corn, fish, meat and so on. The weekly Saturday market of the medieval period was no longer adequate for the town's needs and by the 1590s we begin to find reference to a market on Mondays too. Manchester must have been very congested on market days. It was a market place for the surrounding smaller towns and villages as well, and was sufficient of a draw for traders from as far afield as Warrington and Rochdale to set up stalls, despite the heavier fees and tolls paid by such 'foreigners'.

John Speed's map of 1610 is one of the earliest of the County Palatine of Lancashire and includes Salford Hundred, identifying towns and villages. (Image in public domain, via Wikimedia Commons)

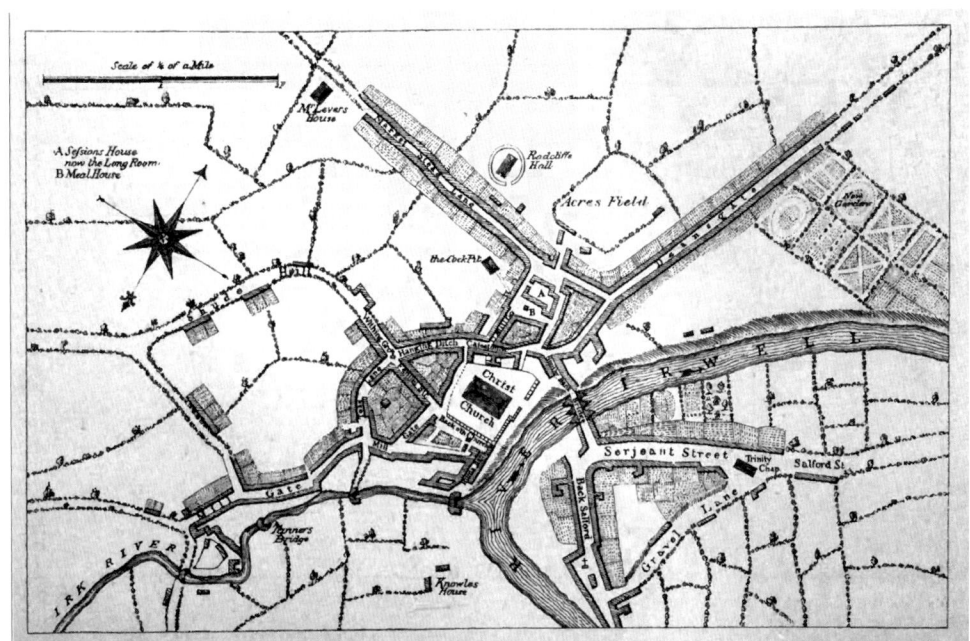

Plan of Manchester in 1650 First published when Casson and Berry used it to accompany their map of the town in 1746, it has been reproduced many times since. Unlike that printed in 1746 this version has street names added. (Image courtesy of Chetham's Library)

References to an 'old market place' at the cross are joined by those to a new market place between the bottom of Market Sted Lane and St Mary's Gate close to the Conduit House. As in almost all successful markets in growing towns, the ground of the market place itself was valuable real estate. Stallholders increasingly sought to turn temporary structures into permanent stalls, and eventually these became fixed shops. Buildings encroached upon the market place, gradually reducing its extent, and by 1700 the medieval market place had almost disappeared. As the market grew but space diminished, traders and their stalls spilled over into surrounding streets causing obstruction and damage to property. Already in the later sixteenth century the court leet was trying to rationalise and control the chaos by allotting specialist areas for traders. For example, bread sellers were told that their proper approved market location was in Smithy Door, not beside the market cross. Butchers were a particular problem: they had their slaughter-houses in the Shambles but could be found trading in both the market places alongside 'foreigners' from other towns and villages. Little wonder, since there were a huge number of butchers with market stalls – in 1599, some 39 traded from 50 stalls. This supports the notion that Manchester provided a market for basic foodstuffs for the surrounding countryside and not just for the town itself.

Apart from congestion, urban growth brought other problems, most notably those connected with sanitation and water supply. The richer households had outside privies, the 'lytle howse', which sometimes drained into middens or were built directly over the numerous natural or artificial watercourses into which they discharged their contents, such that these were effectively open sewers. Other householders made do as best they could. For all, the real problem was disposal of effluent and waste, and private dunghills were common, often a nuisance to neighbours and an unwelcome encroachment on the streets. The jurors frequently ordered that such dunghills be removed, but repeated references in the court leet records to such nuisances suggest that their orders were ignored. There were also public dunghills, including one on the site of the present day St Ann's Square. The court leet sought to enforce seemingly innumerable orders regarding the placement and repair of privies, especially when these were located too close to the street. The general recommendation was that barrels or tubs should be placed under the seat. A typical example is from October 1618, when the jury ordered that 'William Crompton shall cause some wodden or other vessel to bee sett and placed under a privye or place of easement belonginge to his howse and abutting upon the highe streete so as ye Dounge fallinge from ye said privye be nor noisome nor offenceue to his neighbors nor to anye other ye passengers yt waye'.[12] The contents of such vessels were commonly emptied into the Irwell, many householders habitually tipping their tubs from Salford Bridge. Even in the eighteenth century inhabitants were still building privies over town ditches and pouring excrement into the river. Indeed, such insanitary practices persisted well into the industrial era.

Even more than sanitation, the problems of water supply affected all ranks of society. The main source of water for domestic use was the 'Conduit'. Water ran via a pipeline from springs (still commemorated in the street names Fountain Street and Spring Gardens) down Market Sted Lane to a Conduit House in the market place. This water supply was established by private benevolence and maintained by bequests as well as by special leys, or levies on the town's inhabitants. Frequent references to the conduit appear in the court leet records: it was, for example, 'one speciall ornament of the towne', a phrase redolent of civic pride. But the pipeline and conduit were in constant need of repair and the supply of water was never adequate. Water was rationed by custom in order of precedence; each householder had his 'cale' or place in the order of drawing water. The difficulty of ensuring that this custom was observed is reflected in the repeated references to its infringement in the records of the court leet. Attempts were made to control use by limiting the size of the vessels individuals could bring to carry the water, and by placing a time restriction on its use: for example, the court decreed in October 1581 that 'no person or persons shall convey any water between nine a clock in the evening and six a clock in the morning'.[13] Eventually in 1586 the conduit was fitted with lock and key and an official elected to 'kepe the kayes of the Condite' and to ensure that in spring and summer water was drawn only between six and nine in the morning and three and six in the afternoon.[14] The water supply problem did not improve in this period and, while there were other public sources of water, such as 'the pumpe in Deanesgate' and another by Hanging Ditch, and some of the wealthier inhabitants had their own private pumps or wells, the conduit remained essential, and was used by all at some time or another.

How were the various offices and actions of the court leet financed? There was no regular system of local taxation in this period. In addition to fines, customary rates or 'leys' were levied as the need arose, although by the seventeenth century certain activities were financed by more systematic taxation. This was the case with the relief of the poor. The Elizabethan Poor Law of 1601 had laid a duty on the churchwardens and overseers of each parish to raise a poor rate to pay for a 'stock of flax, hemp, wool, thread, iron and other necessary ware and stuff to set the poor on work'. The court leet assumed a role in administering this parish or 'poor's' stock, although the churchwardens of the collegiate church and the overseers of the poor had responsibility for levying the poor rate. The constables were unpaid officials but any expenses connected with their work were paid for by a local rate or 'ley' ordered by the court leet. At first these were occasional but by the seventeenth century the wages of the deputy constable and the beadle became regular charges on the town. Nonetheless a large proportion of the town's expenditure remained irregular, raised according to need, such as in 1612, for example, when the conduit head was in disrepair and in 1615 when a ley was levied for the provision of 'ladders, buckets, hooks and ropes' to fight fires in the town. Responsibility for assessing the liability of inhabitants and for the actual collection of the town's leys was in the hands of the *miselayers* and *misegatherers*. Unpaid and elected annually, these must have been among the least desirable offices of the court leet.

Poor relief and the plague

Although we know something about the wealthy inhabitants of Manchester, the lives of the poorest townsfolk remain obscure to us. The court leet records throw little light on either the numbers or the lives of the poor and, moreover, at first sight the evidence suggests that the wealthy did little to alleviate the sufferings of the needy in their midst. In Lancashire as a whole during the sixteenth and seventeenth centuries, charitable bequests were fewer and less generous than in many other counties. Most were for educational or religious purposes, with only around 20 per cent going to the household relief of the poor. Nevertheless, in Manchester and Salford generosity to the poor was above the county average with over a quarter of bequests being for the relief of poverty.[15] For example, George Clarke, a rich haberdasher who died in the 1630s, left £60 for the making of 120 woollen coats for the poor and £40 to be distributed at his funeral. Most significantly he left property worth £2,000 to be held in trust as an endowment for the 'succor, ayd or releife of such poore, aged, needie or impotent people … as dwell within the said towne of Manchester'. One of the greatest benefactors was Humphrey Booth the Elder (1580–1635), a rich and pious fustian merchant who by a deed of feoffment in 1630 granted to trustees the management of lands which were then fields and are now covered by buildings around Piccadilly and Oxford Street. The deed stated that the income from these lands should be used for the relief of poor, aged or impotent persons dwelling in the town of Salford, and Booth's Charity, as it became known, made small grants of money and provided clothing and blankets for the poor. Booth was precise in his instructions. His will provided that as many woollen coats should be given to the poor as would equal his years at death. These coats were to be 'four yards apiece and dyed black'.[16]

Such bequests to the poor were infrequent in Manchester wills. This fact should not be taken to signify a low level of poverty in the town or an absence of charitable feeling among the rich. Informal face-to-face giving was common among the 'middling sort' who predominated in Manchester and Lancashire at this date, but such 'ad hoc' generosity does not appear in the record. However, in this benevolence there would have been a determined effort to distinguish between the local poor and the economic migrants often complained of by contemporaries. For example, in 1602 the jury of the court leet ordered that 'noe Burges or inhabitant in this towne shall Receave into theire howse or Howses or sett [i.e. let] any Rowmes unto any Strangers suspected to be poore and not hable

Shambles Square The Old Wellington Inn is a remarkable survival. Originally a two-storey building dating from around 1550, a third floor was added in the seventeenth century. Together with Sinclair's Oyster Bar dating from the eighteenth century, these buildings survived the Blitz. When the area around them was redeveloped in the 1960s, both structures were jacked up and secured on a steel and concrete foundation. They became part of a square behind Marks and Spencer. In 1996, unlike the modern buildings around them, they survived the IRA bomb. However, it was decided to move the buildings to make way for the redevelopment of the Marks and Spencer site. This time the Old Wellington Inn was completely disassembled and both structures were moved to a new location near the Cathedral. Originally the two buildings were adjacent but in their new home they have been oriented in an L-shaped configuration. (Shambles Square photo above by Richerman via Wikimedia Commons. Photo of 1960s redevelopment, below, courtesy of Terry Wyke)

to maynteane them selves and their familie without the consent of the Steward, Bororeeve, Constables and forman of the Jurie'.[17] We cannot be sure how far such orders were complied with, but we do know the problem persisted. A generation later, in 1629, the court leet appealed to the assize judges at Lancaster for advice on how far the settlement of strangers could be curtailed, since the town's 'great Provisions for the poore' had become 'such a motive and invitacion of Strangers that are poore and weake in estate as the Towne is att this present soe pestred & overburthened as the native Poore is wronged of that provision w[hi]ch was intended onely for them'.[18] This was a common theme in seventeenth-century poor relief, only partially resolved by legislation in 1662, which laid responsibility for the maintenance of such persons on their parish of settlement. The very openness of Manchester to newcomers must have made this a more acute problem than in less wealthy towns or in those that had guild restrictions.

The poor and lowly appear in the records most obviously at times of crisis. They suffered disproportionately from epidemic diseases such as bubonic plague and were the first affected in years of dearth. Indeed evidence for the poor is found most readily in the burial registers, especially during epidemics. On 16 April 1645 the parish registers record the burial of Marie Bowker aged 20, the daughter of a husbandman living on Long Millgate. Her mother Jane was buried on 27 April and her 14-year-old sister Margaret two days later. Other family members died and eventually, on 4 May, Marie's father Peter was buried. This was the beginning of the last and worst epidemic of bubonic plague to visit Manchester: the Bowker family were among the first victims. There had been previous epidemics in the 1580s and 1590s, but those of 1605 and 1645 were the most severe. It has been estimated that in 1605 over one-quarter of the population may have perished, and in 1645 the epidemic was even worse, perhaps killing as many as one-third of the townspeople. Those were truly terrible years. At times of plague the court leet enacted a number of measures. Infected persons were to be removed to 'pesthouses' on Collyhurst Common: thatched wooden huts in which medical attendants paid on the constables' accounts cared for plague sufferers. Afflicted households might be boarded up, and red crosses painted on the doors. The inhabitants within were thus quarantined, and a special sick tax was raised to pay for their food and provisions. As the number of plague deaths rose burials commonly took place in the plague pits at Collyhurst. The plague was no respecter of rank but the wealthy were more able to escape its reach by removing themselves to the country. For those who remained the epidemic proved particularly virulent in the more crowded parts of the town. The death rate was highest among residents of high-density housing at the back of Market

Place, while on Long Millgate, where the Bowker family lived, over half of households experienced two or more deaths. In contrast, the figure for Smithy Door was just 8 per cent. There the wealthy residents were among those fortunate enough to quit Manchester for the duration of the epidemic.[19]

Plague was often regarded as a judgment from God, but religious uncertainties were many. The sixteenth and seventeenth centuries were a period of religious upheaval and conflict. After the Protestant reformation of the 1530s Lancashire acquired a reputation as a stronghold of the old religion, Roman Catholicism, but the textile district in and around Manchester did not share this traditional allegiance. Indeed, the opposite was the case, for here Protestantism was soon embedded among the population and, within a few decades, nonconformity was emerging. Puritan preachers were influential in the Manchester area from the 1590s onwards, and by the 1630s nonconformist and dissenting congregations were starting to appear.

This probably had much to do with the links brought by trade, especially with London and other clothing districts such as Yorkshire, and historians recognise a close link between nonconformity and merchant and trading activities in areas such as south-east Lancashire. Many prominent local families were Puritan (or 'godly', as they would have put it) in their beliefs and behaviour. This generally meant the nurturing of habits of sobriety and thrift, and sometimes a refusal to conform to the practices of the established Anglican Church. Private belief fed into public action in a variety of ways. It sometimes involved a clash with authority, such as when members of prominent clothier families including the Tippings, the Mosleys and the Booths were prosecuted at the consistory court in Chester for refusing to kneel at communion. There was a degree of public humiliation in this, so the beliefs must have been deeply held, but such actions attracted the support of 'friends' right up to the top of local society. Figures as prominent as Sir Nicholas Mosley publicly defended nonconforming clergy, while others made private bequests to dissenting ministers in their wills. In turn, this strong tradition of Protestant nonconformity in the area fed into political support for the cause of parliament in the civil wars of the 1640s.

Manchester during the Civil Wars

The breakdown of relations between king and parliament that led to the outbreak of civil war had become complete and irrevocable by 1642, though historians trace its immediate causes back into the 1620s and longer-term patterns into the sixteenth century. Once attitudes on both sides had hardened to the point where armed conflict broke out, people were increasingly forced to take sides. While the majority of ordinary people may have remained impartial, or even indifferent, few in the higher ranks of local society could do so. The gentry of Cheshire sought neutrality but before long were compelled by events to choose allegiances. While many factors were involved, religious affinity played a key role in determining the loyalty of leading families and individuals. Lancashire was more divided by religion than any other English county: it has been calculated that as many as two-thirds of the Royalist gentry families in Lancashire were Roman Catholic, and that of the county's gentry families with Parliamentarian sympathies almost three-quarters were Puritan.[20] Thus political and religious divisions were ranged in stark opposition on the battlefield. The towns and villages of the Salford hundred, including Manchester, were that part of Lancashire where Puritan sympathies were strongest and the gentry of the Manchester and Bolton districts were heavily pro-parliament in the civil war. Where the gentry led, other social groups followed – clothiers and other traders, textile workers and yeoman farmers. Although there was a Royalist faction in Manchester the town as a whole stood strongly for parliament.

Manchester saw some of the earliest military action in England, a month before the king raised his standard in August 1642 and the war was officially declared. Royalist forces in the county quickly busied themselves securing control of ammunition wherever they could, and it was known that ten barrels of gunpowder were stored in the college buildings at Manchester, owned by the earls of Derby since the dissolution in 1547. The sixth earl was the county's most powerful landowner, and a devoted supporter of Charles I. His son, Lord Strange, wanted to prevent the ammunition falling into parliamentarian hands and first attempted diplomacy. He arrived before the town in July 1642 with a small force, hoping to take it and secure the armaments. This failed. He reinforced his army and, immediately after war was declared, laid siege to Manchester in September. It must have appeared an easy target and a worthwhile prize – the only major town in the county not held by the Royalists, and with all that ammunition to be gained. The town was not fortified in any way and there were no troops to defend it.

However, these defensive deficiencies were quickly remedied following the engagement of a German military engineer and mercenary soldier called John Rosworm, who directed the construction of mud walls, and the placement of posts with chains across street ends to block a cavalry advance. Twenty-two prominent townsmen guaranteed Rosworm's fee and although he was initially retained for six months, the value of his services ensured that he remained for six years. Rosworm's hasty work on the defences was accompanied by the arrival of local gentry with bands of their tenants, come to resist the expected Royalist onslaught. Up to 2,000 men poured in from the surrounding countryside, armed with muskets, pikes and staves. Lord Strange had mustered four troops of horse and one of dragoons with bands of foot soldiers, the total force variously estimated at between 2,000 and 5,000 men. On Sunday 15 September 1642 they divided and one section, under Lord Molyneux, occupied Salford (which was pro-Royalist) while Strange took up quarters at Alport Lodge at the southern end of Manchester, home of the Royalist sympathiser Sir Edward Mosley, and placed his cannon to point along Deansgate.

The fighting began in earnest the following day. Most of the action took place at Salford Bridge and at the southern end of Deansgate. Tenants of Ralph Assheton of Middleton, who manned the town's only cannon, defended the latter. Rosworm led a group of defenders at Salford Bridge, using the high ground of the parish churchyard to good advantage. Other strongly defended points were Market Sted Lane, Long Millgate and Hunts Bank. Fierce fighting took place as Strange endeavoured to make his way up Deansgate. Several houses and barns were burned and there was close hand-to-hand fighting in which over one hundred Royalists were said to have lost their lives. A Royalist assault on Salford Bridge on the same day was easily repulsed. Fighting continued on and off for a further four days until Strange was forced to withdraw his troops, after an exchange of prisoners. It is estimated that around 200 men died in the siege of Manchester, the great majority of them on the Royalist side. Had the town been taken in 1642 the whole of Lancashire would have fallen into Royalist hands, but instead Manchester became the parliamentarian headquarters for the county for the remainder of the war, with troops permanently garrisoned in the town.[21]

Manchester witnessed no further major fighting, but the effects of civil war on the life of the town were marked. Trade was dislocated and the lodging of troops may well have encouraged the spread of disease, encouraging the plague outbreak of 1645. Lancashire as a whole was badly hit by the civil war years. Interruption of trade was accompanied by food shortages, destitution and disorder. As early as October 1642 the House of Commons discussed the 'great Increase of Poor within the Town of Manchester, and other several Places in Lancashire, by reason of the unavoidable Decay of Trade occasioned by the unhappy Distractions of these Times'.[22] The siege and plague together made this a dark period indeed: the gap in the record of court leet proceedings between 1641 and 1647 was no doubt due to the impact of civil war. During the Commonwealth period the town, with its record of loyalty to the parliamentary cause, received a surprising reward. In 1654 Oliver Cromwell undertook a modest reform of the electoral process, and granted Manchester the right to elect MPs for the first time in its history. The town was represented in the parliaments of 1656 and 1657, but on the Restoration of Charles II in 1660 it was promptly stripped of the privilege. Parliamentary representation was not to be restored until 1832 when Manchester was by that time the largest provincial town in Britain.

Manchester in 1660

Despite the impact of war and plague in the 1640s, by the 1660s signs of rapid and sustained revival were becoming clear. In 1660 Manchester was easily the largest and most populous town in Lancashire. Hearth tax returns for 1664 suggest there were at least 820 households in the township of Manchester and a further 248 across the Irwell in Salford. Taking a mean household size of 4.5 to 5 persons, we arrive at a population for Manchester of around 3,900 with a figure for Salford of about 1,180. Thus we can put the combined population of the twin towns at over 5,000.[23] It is extremely likely that the hearth tax returns underestimated the number of households, so this may be a conservative estimate. At any rate, on the same calculation the next largest town in Lancashire was Wigan, with 458 households and an estimated population of around 2,175. No other town in the county had figures in excess of 2,000. However, in the urban hierarchy of the broader North West, Manchester was still well behind Chester which, with a population of around 8,000, remained as it had been for centuries the most important city in the region.

The region itself was still, in relative terms, economically underdeveloped, although there are indicators that this situation was improving a little over earlier assessments. In a ranking of the wealth of counties calculated according to the hearth tax returns of 1662, Lancashire emerges 30th out of a list of 40, a significant improvement upon its position almost at the bottom of the list 120 years before.[24] We can reasonably speculate that the relative wealth of Manchester and its hinterland contributed much to this advance. The hearth tax returns are the most frequently used indicator of urban populations in the seventeenth century but a ranking of 42 towns derived from these returns places Chester 19th in size and Manchester too small to be on the list at all. There have been other calculations, however, which have included Manchester on the list of larger urban populations circa 1670, and according to these the town may have been the fifteenth largest town in England, some way down the national rankings but growing fast.[25]

Manchester may have almost doubled in population since 1543, which must have affected the topography of the town substantially. It is unfortunate that we have no reliable map of early modern Manchester. Christopher Saxton, the greatest of all sixteenth-century cartographers, spent four days in 1596 making a survey of the town at the request of his host John Dee, the extraordinary polymath, advisor to Queen Elizabeth, and warden of Christ's College between 1595 and 1608. The resulting map, if it were ever to be discovered, would be an invaluable addition to our knowledge and, indeed, to the history of English mapmaking. However, we do have a plan that purports to show Manchester in 1650. Its provenance is unclear and the present plan first saw the light of day when Casson and Berry used it to accompany their map of 1746 (discussed in more detail below). The 1650 map may have been the product of a survey conducted at the behest of the court leet in the 1660s, although conceivably it might even have a relationship to Saxton's missing map. Equally it may be an imaginative invention of John Berry for his 1746 map. Whatever its exact origin, it is a plausible portrayal of the town at the time of the civil war.[26] Together with other evidence it helps us to construct a picture of continued urban development along existing medieval streets, chiefly Deansgate, Long Millgate and Market Sted Lane. Withy Grove and Shude Hill were starting to become built up but there was still comparatively little development outside the old medieval core clustered around St Mary's, the great collegiate church. There were only a few streets and there was no need for houses to be numbered. Manchester was a compact and congested place in which to live.

However, an impression of little change would be misleading, for there had been much infilling of the long narrow burgage plots behind the main streets, as agricultural activity gave way to more strictly urban uses. Orchards were built over, animals were less likely to be accommodated in lands behind the street frontage, and workshops and warehouses began to occupy backlands. This was now a busy town with four distinct market areas (including a fish market and an apple market), two market days per week, and three annual fairs. It was still almost exclusively a settlement of timber-framed buildings, of which the only surviving example is the celebrated Old Wellington Inn (or the Shambles). In 1660 this building stood at the corner of Market Sted and the Shambles (today, off the St Mary's Gate end of New Cathedral Street). It was raised 30 feet into the air and placed on a concrete plinth during the redevelopment of the 1960s, survived the IRA bomb blast of 1996 when the modern buildings around it cracked and crashed to the ground, and has now been moved to a more congenial site near the cathedral in Hanging Bridge Street. The building we now see is merely a fragment of a much larger property which once comprised two warehouses, a brewhouse and a kitchen probably arranged around a courtyard to the rear. It was originally a two-storey structure, built about 1550, the third storey being added in the mid-seventeenth century. We know that in 1660 Edward Byrom, a prosperous linen draper, ran his business from this building. His townhouse was on nearby Hanging Ditch.[27]

Byrom's occupation brings us back to the question of Manchester's economic character at this time. Until the eighteenth century the term 'linen draper' was generally applied to urban merchants in the fustian trade. As we have seen, the fustian trade had begun to supersede the wool trade in Manchester by the 1620s and, since these lighter cloths provided the best return for investment, as the seventeenth century progressed large fortunes were made by the likes of the Chetham brothers. As elsewhere in England the main reason why some towns expanded and grew wealthy in this period was trade and commerce. But as well as being a commercial centre, Manchester was also a manufacturing town with a variety of crafts and occupations. The evidence of the marriage entries in the parish registers of St Mary's between 1653 and 1660 reveals that over 61 per cent of bridegrooms were employed in domestic and craft manufacturing, a far higher proportion than in the villages of the Manchester parish. Textile manufacturing and finishing, especially pure linens and fustians, were the major sources of employment. The largest single occupational group was the handloom weavers. Others engaged in textiles included feltmakers, bleachers, shearers, and clothdressers.[28] This was over a century before the factory age. Yet it is clear that industrial production was already deeply entrenched in the economy and society of the towns and villages of south-east Lancashire. The Manchester of 1660 sat at the heart of a regional economy that revolved around cloth production. As early as 1642 the town had been described as 'the very London of those parts, the liver that sends the blood into all the countries thereabouts'.[29] Manchester merchants led the trade and the town itself had become a centre of production. The seeds of future greatness had been sown.

4

'The greatest mere village in England': roots of industrial revolution, 1660–1780

THE CENTURY or so after 1660 was a time of unprecedented and dramatic change in Manchester. At the end of this period cloths made purely from cotton were being manufactured and marketed by Manchester merchants for the first time, and the rise of the world market for Lancashire cotton goods had begun. By the close of the eighteenth century this erstwhile country market town, then trading town of regional importance and economic hub of the textile trades in the North West, had become a place of national standing, the greatest of all the provincial cities of the realm, second in population only to London itself, and on the cusp of becoming the world's first industrial city. This chapter will try to explain how and why this remarkable transformation had come about.

At the restoration of the monarchy in 1660 Manchester was already recognised as a trading and manufacturing town of regional importance. It was one of a string of newly expanding inland towns situated in industrialising regions, each catering for a specialised product. Thus, Sheffield was famous for its cutlery production; Birmingham was already a centre of metal manufacturing; Nottingham and Leicester were noted for their hosiery; and Leeds was noted for its woollen textiles. In all of these towns trading of finished goods took place as well as actual manufacturing. In the case of Manchester, fustians and linen predominated. These middle-ranking towns of the seventeenth century were to be the industrial giants of the nineteenth, but their rise was strikingly evident by the mid-eighteenth century. A dramatic shift in the urban hierarchy of England was in progress, whereby the older towns that had dominated provincial society since the Middle Ages (Bristol, Norwich, York) were challenged by a new type of urban centre, typified by Liverpool, Birmingham, Manchester. By the time of the first national census in 1801 the ancient centres had been far outstripped by the upwardly mobile newcomers, and Manchester (with Salford) was the largest urban centre outside London. The urban focus of England had thus shifted decisively northwards, towards the Midlands and North West.

Population growth in Lancashire was a striking aspect of this shift. The county's population rose from about 145,000 in 1664 to almost 430,000 by 1781. Moreover, within the North West itself there was a parallel shift, represented by the declining importance of the medieval city of Chester, which had for centuries been the largest urban settlement in the region. By 1778 Liverpool and Manchester were ranked well ahead of Chester and all other towns in the urban hierarchy of north-west England.[1]

This urban 'revolution' must be seen in the context of the fundamental change in population history that occurred during the eighteenth century. The 'Malthusian' preventive checks that had restricted population growth for millennia had by 1750 ceased to operate. This was a result of rapidly rising productivity, first in agriculture, later in manufacturing, which greatly increased the number of people who could be supported by the land. Real wages rose, the age at marriage fell, and fertility rates increased. A growing stream of migration fed the development of towns and cities. Manchester and Liverpool's demographic growth anticipated this national pattern, indicating the economic advance of the region.

Prior to the first official national census in 1801 we have only partial and indirect evidence of the size of Manchester's population, but there is enough data to give us a reasonable sense of what was happening. From evidence such as the lay subsidy returns and hearth tax records, it is possible to infer that the town's population may have doubled between 1543 and 1664. Yet this was just the beginning. Returns made to the bishop of Chester of the number of families in 1717 suggest that, if we take 4.5 per family as the multiplier (and this perhaps errs on the side of caution) the town had at least doubled in size again in less than half a century, to about 9,000 people. From a lower starting point, Liverpool's growth may have been even more rapid during this period. We do not know how reliable are the bishop's returns of 1717 as an estimate of population. It seems they may overstate the case since the period between 1660 and the early eighteenth century generally is reckoned to have been a time of relative stagnation in national population growth. However, we have

	Houses	Families	Males	Females	Marr'd	Wid'd
Ardwick	47	53	115	127	80	6
Broughton	99	104	205	270	102	14
Bradford	13	17	44	55	32	-
Beswick	2	2	6	4	4	-
Burnage	54	55	147	150	93	3
Blakley	240	270	692	702	469	13
Chorlton row	46	49	103	123	70	7
Cadden	10	11	21	24	19	-
Cheetham	93	107	207	243	103	10
Crumpsall	57	63	160	101	116	6
Chorlton	71	75	176	202	120	11
Droylsden	107	111	376	323	210	0
Didsbury	84	86	260	239	150	7
Denton	111	116	318	279	187	10
Falowfield	15	15	26	34	23	-
Failsworth	223	242	609	664	413	24
Gorton	141	144	403	369	245	15
	1413	1520	4,110	4,127	2596	134

Population Census of Manchester 1773–1774
This was the first detailed census of Manchester's population. It reveals that the majority of the 23,000 inhabitants lived in the township of Manchester in sharp contrast to the smaller numbers in the outer townships even those like Ardwick and Chorlton Row that were contiguous to Manchester. The original hand-written manuscript is in the Chetham's Library. (Image courtesy of Chetham's Library)

much stronger evidence for later in the eighteenth century when a population census conducted during 1773–4 reported a figure of around 23,000 (Salford was at this time the largest of the other townships in the Manchester parish with a population of 4,765).[2] Clearly this had been an era of rapid population growth and the demographic checks of earlier times had lost their power.

Those North West towns most closely involved in the textile trades grew at the fastest rate: Manchester, Blackburn, Bolton, Leigh and Stockport each grew more quickly than the population of the region as a whole. In the eighteenth century, these were the chief towns of central and south-east Lancashire and north-east Cheshire, where fustians and linens dominated textile production and woollens were in decline (as opposed to the Pennine east of Lancashire where woollens predominated, and the lowland west and south-west where linens were most important). This was to be a remarkably durable pattern over time: indeed, there is a striking correlation between the spatial geography of the textile industries of the North West in the mid-eighteenth century and that of the cotton district a hundred years later.[3] The urban growth that was engendered early in central and south-east Lancashire persisted into the industrial era. And the chief textile towns of the nineteenth and twentieth centuries had begun their inexorable rise before all-cotton cloths began to be produced.

The rise of Manchester after 1660

As early as the sixteenth century Manchester, of all these south-east Lancashire towns, had become the most important economically. Unlike the others, it became the centre of a regional and not just a local economy. Furthermore, places of major importance in their own right, such as Bolton, Rochdale and Bury, were themselves increasingly 'satellites' within the constellation of towns centred on Manchester. Later, in the 1840s one perceptive visitor, Leon Faucher, remarked that, 'Nothing is more curious than the industrial topography of Lancashire. Manchester, like a diligent spider, is placed at the centre of the web …' Such regional pre-eminence had its roots more than two centuries earlier: how are we to explain Manchester's rise to pre-eminence after 1660?

To approach this question we must first appreciate changes in our understanding of the term 'industrial revolution'. Historians have revised older conceptions of the industrial revolution as a rapid process that was driven by technology and the adoption of factory production, and which transformed the nation in a few decades on either side of 1800. Rather, the process of industrialisation is now understood as a long-drawn-out affair marked by uneven development between regions and industries, in which some parts of the country underwent a revolutionary transformation while others experienced continuity rather than change, and some former handicraft manufacturing districts went into decline. In this process Manchester was in the vanguard of economic change and became the leading town in what was later recognised as the world's first modern industrial region.

Manchester's seventeenth-century position as the control centre of the North West's textile industries was strengthened by subsequent economic development. Recent thinking about the industrial revolution has emphasised the role of regional specialisation and much research and theoretical speculation have centred on the concept of 'proto-industrialisation' as an explanation. The theory is that there was growth in certain regions of Europe, from the sixteenth century onwards, of rural, home-based manufacturing, which in retrospect can be seen as an early stage or precursor of the urban, factory-based, industrialisation of the late eighteenth and nineteenth centuries.[4]

As we have seen, production in the textile industries of the North West (chiefly wool, linen, fustians) had long been organised on a domestic basis, with spinning and weaving done by families who often combined these pursuits with tending an agricultural smallholding. However, employment patterns developed from the relatively independent relationship of the rural artisans with the merchant clothiers in the seventeenth century (described in the previous chapter) to the 'putting-out' system of the eighteenth century, whereby production became increasingly centralised under the control of merchant manufacturers who eventually developed first workshops, then factory-based, industry. Manchester played the controlling role in the co-ordination of rural production throughout south and east Lancashire and north-east Cheshire. Independent spinners and weavers who worked from home and dealt with the masters on equal terms were a dying breed. The growth of the export trade in fustians and checks, and fluctuations in overseas demand, encouraged this process as Manchester merchants sought to gain greater control over the organisation of production. In effect, they became the employers of a rural labour force: putting out the raw material (and particularly the yarn) to cottage workers, paying by the piece, and then marketing the finished cloth. These merchant-manufacturers, familiar with markets and suppliers and employing large numbers of industrial workers, were the key figures in the process.

Moreover, we should not overlook the fact that towns themselves were the sites of industry well before the advent of steam-powered factories in the later eighteenth century. In textile regions the towns had long been centres for the finishing stages of production (dyeing, bleaching, printing), and in the North West smallware manufacture (ribbons, tapes, and buttons) and silk production were also overwhelmingly urban. As the previous chapter suggested, seventeenth-century Manchester already had its own woollen and linen workshops. And historians who have looked at the available (albeit patchy) evidence from Lancashire suggest that some textile manufacture had become an important *urban* industry in the North West well before the end of the eighteenth century. One area of workshop production that emerged early was smallware weaving, which occupied around one-third of Manchester weavers by the mid-eighteenth century. The so-called 'Dutch' or 'engine' loom, used in ribbon making, was too great a capital cost for most ordinary weavers, but a man with moderate means might be able to afford a number of Dutch looms and set journeymen and apprentices to work in a small workshop.[5]

Despite these industrial functions, the most important role of towns such as Manchester (and pre-eminently Manchester itself) was the marketing of cloth produced in the surrounding countryside and in the town itself. This marketing function, which Manchester had already established by the middle of the seventeenth century, was crucial to the commercial rise of the North West as a whole in the following century, and gave the town its international pre-eminence. It linked producers in each of the textile sub-economies of the North West (the linen, woollen and fustian trades) with London agents as well as national and indeed overseas markets.[6] Manchester was the chief business centre for the whole of the regional economy. It was the conduit through which the textile districts of north-west England connected and interacted with the national economy, and it undoubtedly stimulated the economic development of the whole region.

The precise reasons why Manchester achieved this status are still debated. There is no clear consensus on why this particular town was so important, any more than there is on the no less significant question as to why the Lancashire cotton industry was to become a staple sector of the industrial revolution. Physical resources alone do not explain Manchester's exceptionalism. The town was not unique in its natural advantages of location at the confluence of several (albeit minor) rivers (mostly not suitable to power machinery) or in its famously damp climate or in its proximity to a port for imports of raw material. In any case, until the late eighteenth century most raw cotton was imported through London. It was not until after 1800 that slave-produced North American cotton, imported through Liverpool, became dominant in the English market.[7] Other structural considerations such as the proximity of coalfields were to be key to the consolidating of the initial advantage, but the chief impact of these came later, in the post-1780 era of steam power, after Manchester's advantageous position had already been established. Some have argued that we should look beyond these deterministic arguments about physical location and assets, and instead seek other explanations for Manchester's precocious economic growth up to 1780.

According to this perspective, a more likely explanation might be the town's relatively open society. The absence of a corporation and of craft guilds is often regarded as a positive contribution to Manchester's rising fortunes, and it was a point clearly recognised by contemporaries. In the early eighteenth century Daniel Defoe, in a phrase quoted countless times by writers on Manchester and its history, referred to the town as 'the greatest mere village in England'.

> From hence we came on to Manchester, one of the greatest, if not really the greatest mere village in England. It is neither a wall'd town, city, or corporation; they send no members to Parliament; and the highest magistrate they have is a constable or headborough; and yet it has a collegiate church, several parishes, takes up a large space of ground, and, including the suburb, or that part of the town called over the bridge; it is said to contain above fifty thousand people.[8]

Defoe was wildly wrong in his estimate of Manchester's population but he did identify one of the enduring features of the town, the surviving remnants of manorial administration. It was not unusual for smaller places to be thus governed but the sheer size of Manchester made such a system seem anomalous. Manchester and Birmingham (another place which achieved a comparable dominance in its region and in the control of the specialised industries of its hinterland) were the largest unincorporated towns in the eighteenth century. In Manchester the court leet remained the principal organ of local government, sharing responsibilities with churchwardens and overseers of the poor, the parish vestry and magistrates. This situation prevailed until the latter end of the century when statutory commissioners for particular purposes were appointed, following police and improvement Acts of Parliament in 1765, 1776 and 1792. While some, like Defoe, expressed surprise at this antiquated method of administration, especially as the town grew in size and importance, others saw the absence of a corporation, with the consequent lack of restrictions on trade that could have been imposed by craft guilds, as a positive advantage.

The eighteenth century was a period of declining economic regulation across the nation as a whole. The commercial role of craft guilds as 'closed shops', restricting trade only to their members, went into rapid decline from the early years of the century. Long before their legal abolition by parliament in 1835, such restrictive practices had become unsustainable at law. Furthermore, the long-standing role of the magistracy in wage regulation was repeatedly ignored in defining relationships between masters and employees, and the traditional apprenticeship system, although more durable, was gradually being eroded. This economic deregulation was not planned, and it was not yet a coherent 'free market' philosophy, but it undoubtedly contributed to national economic progress. As already noted, many contemporaries saw Manchester's lack of guild restrictions as a key to its commercial precocity. Its non-corporate status reinforced the 'openness' of its society. A broadside of 1731 concluded that 'The Town of Manchester being no corporation ... is free and open for all Persons whatsoever to set up and exercise any Trade there; and to this the Improvement of the Manufacturing, and flourishing Condition of that town is greatly owing.' Manchester, being free, wrote Lord Kinnoull in 1767, was a place where 'genius had free scope and industry is exerted to the utmost without control, check or interruption'. Later, James Ogden observed that perhaps nothing has more contributed to the improvements in trade here, than the free admission of workmen in every branch, whereby trade has been kept open to strangers of every description, who contribute to its improvement by their ingenuity; for Manchester ... is not subject to such regulations as are made in corporations, to favour freemen in exclusion of strangers: and indeed nothing could be more fatal to its trading interest, if it should be incorporated and have representatives in Parliament.[9]

This was an oft-repeated claim but was it justified? In a non-corporate town the interests of newcomers would not be sacrificed to the privileges of freemen, which would encourage enterprise and permit free entry for migrants. The lack of restrictions may indeed have encouraged technological innovation, as in the ready adoption by Manchester men of the Dutch loom for tapes and ribbons after the Restoration, and this may later have enabled the linen industry to adapt quickly to the introduction of cotton.[10] But the point should not be over-played. Some incorporated towns also expanded as industrial centres (Leeds and Coventry are good examples) and in the process generally abandoned guild restrictions, while the other urban sensation of the early eighteenth century, Liverpool, was itself an incorporated borough with a mayor, aldermen and councillors, guilds, regalia, and all the trappings of 'ancient privilege'. In any case, as merchant entrepreneurs transferred textile production from the towns to the countryside, where producers rarely enjoyed any protection or special privilege, it was largely irrelevant whether or not a town was unincorporated. So perhaps the absence of municipal and guild restrictions, while undoubtedly a factor, should be regarded as *permitting* but not *causing* economic growth.[11] However, what is most interesting is the fact that contemporaries so readily and so repeatedly vaunted the openness of Manchester's society. This suggests they were promoting a particular and distinctive identity for the town.

By the early eighteenth century the image of Manchester in the national consciousness was that of a trading town *par excellence*. Those who purchased 'Manchester Cottons', 'Manchester Gowns' or 'Manchester Breeches' automatically associated the town with textiles and with trade. Travelling dealers or chapmen, also known as 'Manchester Men', with their droves of heavily laden pack horses, journeyed all over England, supplying fairs, markets and retailers, and acting as incidental ambassadors for their town. It soon became clear that Manchester's prosperity depended upon the success of its trade and its traders. It has even been argued that Manchester's 'chief inhabitants' possessed such a 'business mentality' that fostering the commercial success of the town was a deliberate policy of local government. This argument suggests that the absence of guild restrictions was reinforced by a local taxation regime that gave 'tax breaks' to the small business operator in the shape of lower poor rate charges on 'personalty' (stock-in-trade) than on land, thus penalising the landed at the expense of those engaged in trade. Thus, to economic deregulation was added a policy of tax advantages for business, and together they fostered a climate in which there were few impediments to prosperity and expansion.[12]

While a lack of restrictions and the development of a 'business mentality' may have been facilitating factors, there were other reasons contributing to Manchester's success. It was crucial that in the course of the sixteenth and seventeenth centuries the town had developed a specialised role in terms of production and marketing. As it was the economic pivot of its region, the arrival of an appropriately skilled population, the growth of a reputation for a particular product, and the development of a merchandising network, all reinforced this advantage. The market links within and beyond the region, the distribution of market information, capital and credit, all passed through Manchester. The trading links with London, well established since the sixteenth century, facilitated the export of 'Manchester' textiles, including the new fustian fabrics. None of this could have happened without the existence in the town of an experienced and dynamic mercantile class with two centuries of accumulated manufacturing and trading expertise. This strong mercantile tradition was the solid foundation on which much later development was based. However, there was one further, crucial, advantage – the product with which the town was associated. Other industrial towns also specialised in particular products, but it was the successful adoption by Manchester merchants of cotton cloth, with its huge sales potential in terms of domestic and world trade, which was to propel the town and the region to the forefront of industrialism.

The market for cotton goods

In the early eighteenth century cotton accounted for a very small proportion of Britain's textile production. Linens and woollens comprised around three-quarters of exported cloth from these islands. At this time, Indian cotton goods manufactured on hand-powered machinery dominated the world market and were purchased across the globe from Japan to the Americas. Attempts during the eighteenth century to imitate these Indian cloths were to stimulate technological innovations in the manufacture of cotton textiles that eventually achieved a shift in the locus of production from Asia to Europe. This was the most significant feature of a pattern of global economic divergence that saw Europe and North America industrialise and the textile economies of Asia stagnate as the balance of economic power shifted decisively westwards: a pattern in the location of textile manufacture not reversed until the mid-twentieth century.

For most of the period British producers mixed cotton with yarns from other textiles. It was not until the second half of the eighteenth century that all-cotton cloths began to be manufactured. As the market for British-produced cotton goods expanded Manchester was well placed to exploit its potential for wealth creation. The town was already the regional centre of the woollen and linen industries, and continued to be notable for its smallware manufacture and silk weaving, but the trade in with-cotton products now provided the real impetus for expansion. As early as the 1690s cotton was being added to established linen lines to produce cotton-linen checked and striped cloths which appealed to a growing domestic market. The relative importance of cotton among the other textiles manufactured in the region continued to advance during the first half of the eighteenth century, and the central place of Lancashire in the British cotton industry was established long before the first steam-powered mill was built. At the beginning of the eighteenth century cotton was used in textile manufacture in a variety of English locations, including Spitalfields in east London, and Weymouth and other centres in the South West. These areas of production were in rapid decline by the mid-eighteenth century. The water-powered mills of the Derwent Valley in Derbyshire, founded by Richard Arkwright and his competitors from the 1770s onwards, were losing out to Lancashire mills by the early nineteenth century. By this time, apart from the Manchester basin and its immediate surroundings, only in lowland Scotland, with Glasgow as the hub of production and distribution, was there a significant British cotton industry. This remained second only to Lancashire, until it went into decline after 1860. It is no coincidence that both Manchester and Glasgow were previously at the centre of thriving linen industries. The combination of cotton-linen products such as fustians, checks and smallwares with improved printing techniques has been seen as marking the birth of the British cotton industry.[13]

During the eighteenth century cotton fabrics, especially cloth printed with brightly coloured and lively patterns, became fashionable among all social classes in England. This demand for cotton goods had grown during

Indian chintz early eighteenth century Chintz originally referred to glazed calico textiles imported from India and printed with designs featuring flowers, animals and other patterns in a variety of colours. The production process was lengthy and involved separate stages for the dying of each colour with fine details being hand painted. These fabrics were fashionable in Britain as curtains and bedspreads. The name is derived from the Hindi chint, meaning 'spotted or variegated'. (Image courtesy of Cooper Hewitt, Smithsonian Design Museum, Gift of Josephine Howell, via Wikimedia Commons)

the seventeenth century, when calicoes, chintzes and muslins imported from India by the East India Company had been highly desirable fashion items for the rich, for whom they often substituted for more expensive French silks. Soon the Company was aggressively marketing vividly coloured, floral-patterned, checked or plaid clothing and soft furnishings to the middling ranks of society and below. For the consumer the appeal of cotton fabric over wool was not only its potential to take colourful prints and designs, but also its lightness and the ease with which it could be washed and dried. To protect the position of woollens as the dominant textile industry against the new lighter more versatile imported cotton cloths, a campaign was mounted to prohibit the import of Indian textiles. This led to protectionist legislation with Acts of Parliament in 1701 and 1721. The intention was to ban the sale of most Indian textiles to British consumers.

In practice Indian calicoes could not be excluded entirely, but the main impact of the legislation was to stimulate home production to replace imports. The East India Company now concentrated on the import of cotton yarn, on which there was no ban. Neither the spinners nor the weavers in Britain

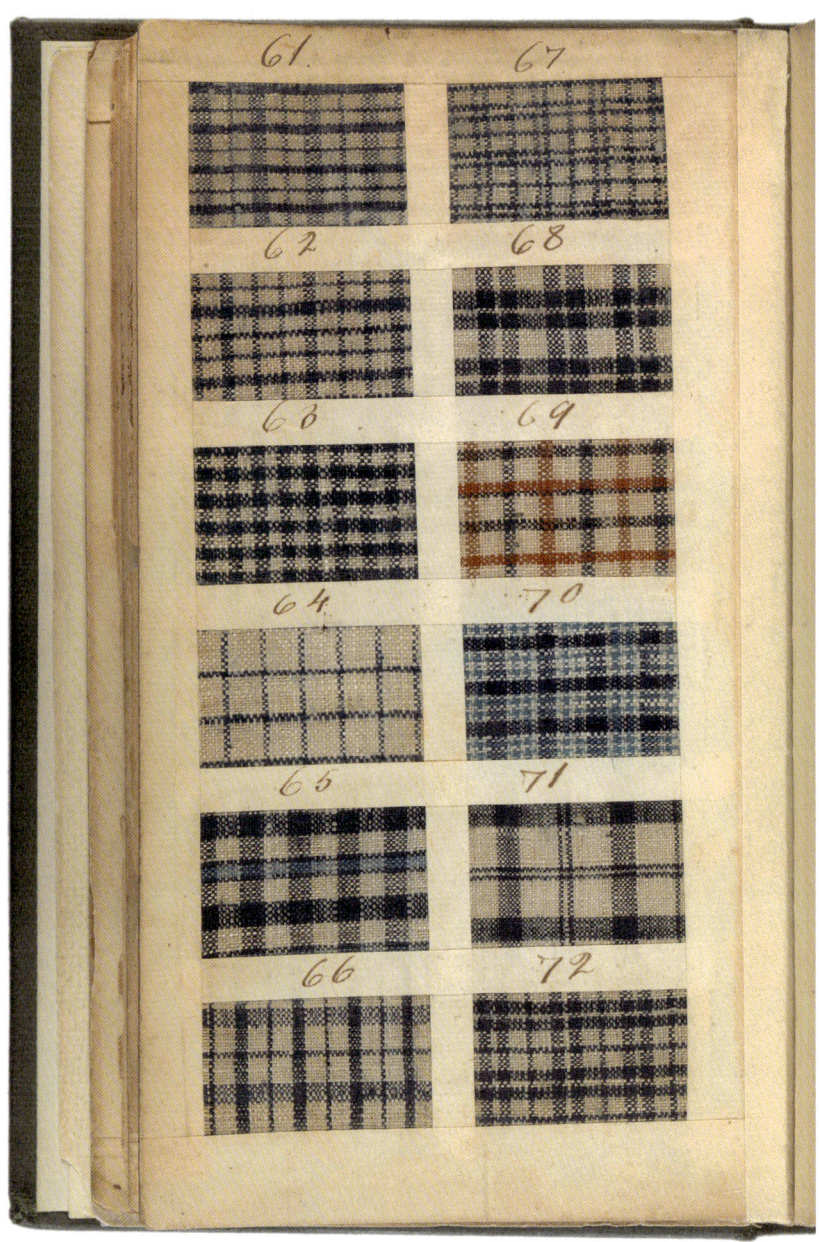

Textile sample book of a Manchester merchant 1771 Swatches of fabric made by the Manchester manufacturing firm of Benjamin and John Bower. The samples were woven with a very fine cotton warp and single, silk weft. Such sample books were an important sales tool especially in the export trade (Image © The Metropolitan Museum of Art/Art Resource/Scala, Florence)

possessed the skill to produce cotton fabrics of a quality comparable to Indian calicoes, whether or not there was a ban on such goods. Therefore, rather than compete for the market in that high-quality product, the home producers at first mixed wool or linen with cotton to make cheaper fabrics. This, of course, was a trade in which Lancashire already specialised. Lancashire's linen-cottons might not have been able to match the quality or the variety of Indian fabrics, but an unintended consequence of the legislation was that it sheltered them from the competition of the superior craftsmen of India.[14] The legality of this 'substitution' of home production for the loss of high quality Indian imports was enshrined in law in 1736 by legislation appropriately known as the 'Manchester Act'. Moreover, the ban on Indian imports of finished cloth stimulated the domestic calico printing industry since the East India Company could still legally import Indian cottons as long as they were for export to colonial and African markets. This was usually after the addition of colourful patterns printed in Britain. Gradually, but markedly, the quality and range of domestic cotton products improved: by the mid-eighteenth century a range of all-cotton cloths was being manufactured in Lancashire, the largest category of these being the all-cotton velvets produced in Manchester, for which the town soon became internationally renowned.[15]

The wardrobe of the mid-eighteenth-century consumer still largely consisted of wool, linen, leather and silk garments, but cottons soon became an item of everyday wear and even maidservants were wearing striped cotton gowns. No less important, in an increasingly consumerist society, was that 'furniture checks' began to compete with woollen hangings for the cheaper sort of covers and curtains.[16] Although technically banned by the 1721 Act, all-cotton textiles began to appear in increasing numbers and variety. As prohibited goods they should have been confiscated and fines imposed, but in practice the law was difficult to enforce and its impact waned. After the middle of the century powerful influence could be brought to bear by some of the newly wealthy cotton producers. When Richard Arkwright sought to export his printed calicoes he found they were subject to twice the excise duty levied on cotton-linen goods. In 1774 he successfully petitioned parliament for the repeal of the Act.[17]

But by then the removal of a largely redundant prohibition was less important than rapid technological change. Inventions such as John Kay's flying shuttle greatly improved the speed and quality of weaving. Later, new spinning machines – James Hargreaves' jenny, Richard Arkwright's water-frame, and Samuel Crompton's spinning mule – overcame technical problems in mechanised production while enabling finer yarns to be spun.[18]

The chief impact of the last invention, the mule, came after 1790 through its adaptability for steam-powered production in factories. Soon the world was buying Manchester goods that approached the quality of cottons produced on the Indian subcontinent but produced with yarn spun on powered machinery at a fraction of the cost of Indian producers. In the event, it was not on the quality of the product alone that the English industrial revolution in cotton textiles was built, but on the inexpensiveness and pace of production.

New technology was crucial, but why was it adopted? It is easy to rely too much on hindsight. We know the outcome of mechanisation, but people at the time did not, and nor could they anticipate the rapidity and scale of change and innovation. So there had to be an immediate financial inducement for manufacturers. It may, indeed, have been England's historically high-wage economy that encouraged its adoption, as a means of saving on labour costs.

Richard Arkwright (1732–1792) Richard Arkwright was arguably the most famous industrialist of the early industrial revolution. His water-powered mill at Cromford in Derbyshire pioneered cotton spinning and in 1782 he built the first cotton mill in Manchester. Portrait by the American artist Mather Brown, 1790. (Image courtesy of the New Britain Museum of American Art, Charles F. Smith Fund, via Wikimedia Commons)

John Kay, Inventor of the Fly Shuttle by Ford Madox Brown, mural in the Great Hall of Manchester Town Hall. John Kay's flying shuttle greatly improved the speed and quality of weaving. This portrayal of his workshop in Bury has him wrapped in a woollen blanket as he escapes from rioting weavers whose jobs were threatened by this new invention. This apocryphal story was widely believed in Victorian times. Kay's flying shuttle can been seen in the background of this image. (Image in public domain, via Wikimedia Commons)

To compete with Indian cotton products on the world market (especially in the fine cloths which were highly labour-intensive) meant that it was essential to undercut on price. One way to reduce production costs would be to cut wages, but the existing wage gap between Britain and India, and the likely resistance to wage cuts in areas such as Lancashire where labour organisation was beginning to stir, made this a less attractive solution than the introduction of new technology. There was even a wage differential with producers in continental Europe. In France, for example, where Rouen and Nantes were textile centres competitive with Manchester, the lower wages paid to textile workers offered less incentive for employers to invest in labour-saving technology, even though French manufacturers were well aware of new machinery such as the spinning jenny.[19] France as well as the rest of Europe soon became an important market for Lancashire's cotton goods.

In 1786 Joseph Smith and Robert Peel speaking on behalf of the Manchester calico printers summed up the main reasons for the success of British producers in overseas markets:

Spinning Jenny One of the key inventions of the early industrial revolution, this is the improved version that was being used in factories by the early nineteenth century. (Image in public domain, via Wikimedia Commons)

> The principal advantage of the English cotton trade arises from our machines both for spinning and printing; by means of these we can spin both cheaper and better, and we can print not only cheaper and better, but we save more than half of the colours that before were wasted. ... With respect to colours and taste, I think we are on a par with any other country.

Indian producers were soon expressing alarm at the quality and cheapness of the products being sold through Manchester. In 1783 the East India Company sent three boxes of samples to Bengal, 'the produce of a manufacture that has lately been set up at Manchester'. The company's representative was impressed, remarking on the 'great degree of perfection to which this manufacture is already arrived although at present only in its infancy; the prices which are 20% under our own, are circumstances which cannot but justly alarm us.'[20]

Manchester, cotton and slavery

Looking forward to the nineteenth century Manchester's prosperity was to depend on the cotton industry and most of the raw cotton imported through Liverpool to supply Lancashire's mills came from the slave plantations of the southern USA. Great wealth flowed from this miracle product of industrialism and the extent of this wealth owed much to its roots in slave labour and had its origins in the Atlantic slave trade. This much was in the future. But as we shall see below slavery and slave ownership also played a part in making some in the town very rich even before the factory age of industrialism.

A sign of the town's growing wealth may be found in the tax returns of households paying stamp duty on silver plate in 1757. When the returns are aggregated by town, they can be used as an indicator of urban prosperity, represented by 'genteel and middle-class residence', rather than straightforward numbers of people. While the places with the largest numbers of those paying silver plate duty were still the ancient cities of Bristol, Norwich, York, and Exeter, Manchester came fifth in a list of over 130 towns, ahead of places such as Bath, Newcastle, Oxford, Chester and numerous others. Liverpool also was placed high on the list.[21] Manchester was acquiring a reputation as a place where money was to be made. An indication of this was the willingness of gentry families to pay premiums of up to £500 for their younger sons to become apprentices in Manchester mercantile houses.[22]

Trade and manufacture produced a class of newly successful business families with wealth and status, just as a century earlier the first generation of clothiers, such as the Chethams and the Mosleys, had risen to prominence. An early example of this new business class was Edward Byrom (died 1711), the linen draper who occupied the Old Shambles in Market Place. His elder son, also called Edward, inherited the business and later, in 1735, as proprietor of the Mersey and Irwell Navigation was responsible for the construction of Manchester's first quay on land owned by the family and fronting the river Irwell. Meanwhile the family's wealth had enabled the younger of Edward's sons, John Byrom (1692–1763), to be educated at Cambridge University, where he created a form of shorthand and developed his propensities as a poet. The rest of the Byrom lands at the south end of Deansgate were later developed as a residential estate around St John's church, founded by John's son, another Edward, in 1768. A less well-known example is James Bayley (1674–1753), a prominent Manchester merchant whose father had been a silk weaver in the town. His eldest son converted the family inheritance into a landed estate and lived the life of a country gentleman, but the younger sons stayed in trade and their sons in turn were check manufacturers and cotton merchants.

More wealthy but less typical were the Touchets. Their family business was founded by Thomas Touchet (1679–1745), a pinmaker of Warrington, who married well, moved to Manchester, became a manufacturer of linen and cotton goods, and emerged as the town's wealthiest merchant. Thomas's younger sons continued the business in Manchester while Samuel (1705–1773), his eldest son, represented the firm in London. Samuel Touchet's business career prospered, with interests in the import of raw cotton from the Levant and the West Indies, and linen yarn from Europe. He was so successful with the importing of cotton that the other Manchester manufacturers suspected him of seeking a monopoly. His ambitions in this regard are unclear, but an attempted alliance in the early 1740s with Lewis Paul, inventor of the first roller-spinning machine, could have given him a monopoly of cotton spinning by means of powered machines. In any case he was exceptionally wealthy, especially as his business interests diversified during the 1750s into shipping, insurance broking, speculation in naval prizes, and the sugar and slave trades. Like many eighteenth-century merchants with wide connections and considerable assets abroad, he became a government contractor and financier, eventually pursuing a political career. Long before entering parliament he represented Lancashire's commercial interests in London and led parliamentary agitations such as that in 1751 for a bounty on checked and striped linens.[23]

The Touchets were Unitarians, and several were trustees of the Cross Street Chapel. Although non-conformity in general and the Cross Street Chapel in particular was to be associated with the abolitionist movement there were several families connected with the chapel in the eighteenth century that had slave trade interests. Apart from the Touchets another notable example was the Hibbert family. Robert Hibbert (1684–1762) began as a linen draper but the family business he founded grew to supply cotton pieces for Liverpool slavers. The Hibberts are a prime example of how slavery could transform an otherwise modest mercantile concern into a successful business dynasty with all the perquisites of status and power that came with it. Robert's eldest son Thomas Hibbert (1710–1780) strengthened the firm's commercial interests by his exploits in Jamaica, becoming part of the island's colonial elite and one of its most important slave traders. He built an imposing residence in Kingston and purchased a 3000 acre estate at Agualta Vale, which he turned over for sugar cultivation. Thomas's brother Robert Hibbert senior (1717–1784) was a prominent West-India merchant in Manchester. The family connection with Jamaica continued into the next generation and George Hibbert (1757–1837) became the most important Jamaica merchant in Britain, Member of Parliament and chief spokesman for the Caribbean slavers opposing the abolition of slavery in British possessions, which was finally enacted by statute in 1833.[24]

The involvement of the Touchets and Hibberts in slave owning and the slave trade invites questions about the connections between Manchester, cotton and slavery in the eighteenth century. To what extent did the cotton industry rely on the labour of African slaves before the advent of American slave plantations in the years following the War of Independence, and what were the links between cotton exports from Britain and the Atlantic slave trade prior to its abolition in British ships in 1807?

By early nineteenth century the chief source of raw cotton for the British cotton industry was the slave-plantation economy of the southern states of the newly formed USA. Britain's dominance of world trade in the nineteenth century was in great part a consequence of the phenomenal growth in its exports of cotton piece goods most of which were manufactured in Lancashire's mills and exported via Manchester. All those involved in the Lancashire cotton industry and in Manchester's role as the centre of the world market in cotton were ultimately dependent upon the institution of slavery and it has been argued that such predominance would not have been achieved without the enslavement of Africans.[25] For much of the eighteenth century the situation was somewhat different. Cotton had yet to assume its critical role in the British industrial revolution and the plantations of Virginia, South Carolina and the other slave states had yet to become the chief source of supply. Moreover, before the 1790s most imports of raw cotton did not involve the use of slave labour. The Levant was a key area of production, especially the Ottoman Empire, which supplied around 20% of cotton imports to Great Britain in the 1780s.[26] Production in this semi feudal economy was by small farmers or free labourers. However, increasing imports of raw cotton came from British possessions in the West Indies. This did involve slave labour. Jamaica, Grenada and Dominica exported cotton throughout the eighteenth century although sugar remained a more profitable investment. Islands with fewer sugar plantations had turned to cotton by the 1760s, most notably Barbados. British merchants were also able to buy from plantation owners in the French Caribbean island of Saint-Domingue where supply outstripped the demand from the French cotton industry. Another source of slave-produced cotton was Brazil. Although Brazilian cotton did not arrive at British docks until after 1780 the Portuguese colony soon became a major supplier. By 1790 raw cotton imported from the West Indies and Brazil had overtaken supplies from the Levant and slavery had assumed its pivotal role in supplying raw material for Britain's cotton industry.

From the earliest days of cotton production in Britain a significant proportion was destined for overseas markets. By the 1780s most British cotton exports were to Europe, North America, the West Indies and Africa.[27] Did any of this involve the slave trade? As early as the sixteenth century Portuguese traders had

Monument of the late Thomas Hibbert, Esq., at Agualta Vale Hibbert's imposing funeral urn was located on a promontory overlooking his estate. The plantation remained in the Hibbert family until after slavery in British possessions was abolished in 1833. The Hibberts owned other slave plantations in Jamaica. This picture is from James Hakewill, *A Picturesque Tour of the Island of Jamaica* (1825). (Image in public domain, via Wikimedia Commons)

sold Indian textiles in West Africa in exchange for slaves. Traders from other European nations followed suit. By the second half of the eighteenth century British producers could sell cotton goods made in Britain as well as cottons from India on African markets. British and Indian textiles constituted around two thirds of all British exports to Africa at this time.[28] Much of this commerce supported the 'triangular trade' in which raw cotton was imported from the Americas to Europe where it was used to manufacture printed cotton goods for export to Africa in exchange for slaves who were then transported to plantations across the Atlantic. Thus European producers including those in Manchester were further implicated in slavery and the slave trade.[29]

Manchester was to play a notable part in the history of opposition to the slave trade and slavery, from the famous abolitionist Thomas Clarkson being invited to preach against slavery in the pulpit of the collegiate church in 1787, to the meeting at the Free Trade Hall in 1862 that resolved to send a letter from the workingmen of Lancashire urging the abolition of slavery on President Lincoln during the American Civil War. But there were two sides to this coin. There were always those who campaigned against slavery. But equally, much of the wealth and importance of nineteenth century Manchester, up to the outbreak of the American Civil War in 1861, was derived from the fact that the staple industry and trade of its economy relied on imported raw materials harvested with slave labour. In the eighteenth century the institution of slavery had also helped nurture the embryonic British cotton industry although it was in the decades that followed the 1780s that it was to assume its dominant role. Yet it is also clear that its contribution was increasing before 1780 and, at a time when it was no barrier to respectability to trade in slaves or to be a slave owner, families like the Touchets and the Hibberts achieved commercial success, social status and political prominence through the business of slavery.

The beginnings of industrial Manchester

As the hub of the worldwide trade in cotton Manchester was to become a world-famous commercial centre during the industrial revolution. Indications of this future pre-eminence can be found as early as the 1750s, some time before the introduction of powered machinery. By this date Manchester had already assumed the pivotal role in the sale and distribution of Lancashire's cotton goods, as it had previously been the marketing centre for the region's wool and linen products. However, this time the trade was in what was to become the most important manufactured commodity in the world.[30]

Much of the manufacture of British cotton goods was for the export market. Initially this was a trade dominated by London merchants, but by the 1780s northern firms had seized the initiative from London, notably in textile exports to the lucrative North American market.[31] The export of cotton cloth was to prove extremely valuable to the British economy. As early as 1784 cotton goods constituted 6 per cent of total British exports, even before steam power had been successfully applied to the spinning process. When it did arrive (it took until the 1820s before the power loom began a similar transformation of the weaving process), from the 1790s onwards, machinery that was powered directly by rotary steam engines enabled a spectacular transformation in the cost and amount of yarn being spun. Along with the great economies of scale that could be achieved when such machinery was installed in large factories, combined with the expansion of the area of cotton cultivation possible under the American slave system, this was to have a profound effect: as early as 1804 cotton goods comprised an astonishing 42 per cent of British exports.[32] Manchester was becoming the commercial hub of a global trade in cotton goods. The decades after 1780 undoubtedly witnessed a phenomenal escalation of Manchester's importance in the world. But as this chapter has sought to demonstrate this apparently overnight transformation had its roots in the era before the factory age.

5

Living in eighteenth-century Manchester

During the eighteenth century great fortunes were made from the textile trades in Manchester, and much of this new wealth was invested in the building of elegant streets and squares of stone and brick houses. This new elegance was matched by the social life of the place as, like other prosperous Georgian towns, Manchester became a centre for consumption and display. There were thriving musical and theatrical venues, polite assemblies, reading rooms and coffee houses and other more socially dubious gatherings, for horse racing and cock fighting. There was a lot of new money in Manchester, but it was not spread evenly, and there were repeated food riots and strikes. During this period, Manchester acquired not only its enduring 'brand' as a trading town, but also a reputation as a troublesome place. In particular it gained an unwelcome notoriety as the home of Jacobite sympathisers, being the only town in England to give succour to the Stuart pretender in the rising of 1745.

As it grew in both size and importance, what kind of town was Manchester becoming? When Celia Fiennes, the intrepid lady traveller, visited back in 1698 she had described it thus: 'Manchester Lookes exceedingly well at the Entrance – very substantiall buildings, the houses are not very Lofty but mostly of Brick and stone, the old houses are timber work; there is a very Large Church all stone and stands high soe that walking round the Church-yard you see the whole town.'[1] This suggests the timber-framed town of 1660 was already changing in appearance, as wealthier inhabitants had new houses built. By the second quarter of the eighteenth century there

Whitworth's 'South West Prospect of Manchester and Salford', 1734.
(Image courtesy of Chetham's Library)

had been much more building in brick and stone. However, we cannot be sure of the town's precise development during this period. Surprisingly, there is no surviving authenticated street map of Manchester before that published in 1741 by Casson and Berry. The same publishers produced several further editions of this map. As an additional source of evidence there are two panoramic views or 'prospects': Samuel and Nathaniel Buck's 'South West Prospect' published in 1728; and Robert Whitworth's 'South West Prospect of Manchester and Salford' published in about 1734. The panoramas and maps together confirm the picture of a town that was expanding rapidly.[2] In the 1746 edition of Casson and Berry's map there was incorporated the first known publication of the plan of the town in 1650 (see above, chapter 3). The purpose of including this earlier plan was explicitly to demonstrate the urban transformation that was under way. The 1751 edition of Casson and Berry's map was accompanied by an introduction in which it was claimed that whereas in 1650 there had been 24 streets and lanes in Manchester and Salford, the map now showed some 160 thoroughfares.

The geography of the place had changed very greatly in the century to 1751. As the population increased so did land values, and there were opportunities for speculative development. Burgage plots, laid down during the medieval centuries with their associated courtyards and long gardens, were filled with new building; and empty spaces on existing streets were developed to meet the demands of an expanding town. Fields and country lanes on the outskirts were laid out as streets

St Ann's Church, St Ann's Square Built between 1709 and 1712 using purple-red Collyhurst sandstone, the west tower originally had a three stage cupola that was removed in 1777 and replaced with the upper stage of the tower we see today.
(Image © Carnegie Publishing)

and given urban names. Some of this extended the development beyond the older limits of the town, especially to the south-west. Here, new improvements included residential squares, so characteristic of Georgian urban design. Part of the former Acres Field was laid out as a formal square following the erection of St Ann's church between 1709 and 1712. This square, named after the church, was completed by 1720 and, adorned with formal rows of trees, soon became the most fashionable quarter of town. It was one of the earliest residential squares to appear in any provincial town. Adjacent to the new square, the new and very fashionable King Street led to St James's Square, itself linked to Market Street Lane via Brown Street. Today King Street has the only surviving examples of early eighteenth-century houses built for the wealthier Manchester citizens, notably no. 56 (built around 1700) and nos 35–37, a brick-built house dating from 1736. Such urban growth reflected commercial wealth, as the richest beneficiaries of economic expansion sought a lifestyle they thought appropriate to their newly acquired station in life. Some of these were very grand houses indeed, as the illustrations around the various editions of the Casson and Berry maps were intended to demonstrate.

St Ann's Square and its immediate surroundings were the most impressive urban developments of the early eighteenth century, but new building extended more widely. Deansgate was also being developed as far as Kay (Quay) Street, and the areas of open land behind this main thoroughfare were soon laid out with new residential quarters. Today the area west of Deansgate, which includes John Street, Byrom Street and Quay Street, retains sufficient of its later eighteenth-century fabric to give at least a general impression of the appearance of the Georgian town. Cobden House, a three-storey town house originally built in the 1770s by the Byrom family on the corner of Byrom Street and Quay Street, has the best-preserved interior.[3] Despite this rapid urban expansion, however, the countryside was still in sight. Whitworth's 'South West Prospect' of 1734 shows the river Irwell in the foreground, flowing through a rural landscape. On both sides of the river stretch fields and orchards up to an urban perimeter of impressive properties with walled gardens and gazebos behind the houses in Parsonage Gardens and Spinningfields. The towers of three churches are visible – two of these are Salford Holy Trinity and the Collegiate Church, but the eye is inevitably drawn to the impressive cupola of the newest foundation, St Ann's, and the fashionable residential district that had grown up around it. By contrast, the overcrowded streets and alleyways around the Collegiate Church are hidden from view.

A physical symbol of Manchester's flourishing economy in the early eighteenth century was the Mersey and Irwell Navigation, which gave the town's traders a waterway to the sea thirty miles away. This objective had long been sought, and as early as the 1660s there had been serious proposals for improving the river, but none came to fruition. Eventually, in 1721, an Act of Parliament was obtained to make the Irwell navigable from Hunt's Bank in Manchester to Bank Quay in Warrington. The chief promoters of this scheme were representatives of some of Manchester's leading families, including George Kenyon, Oswald Mosley, Samuel Clowes and Edward Byrom. Work progressed slowly, but by 1736 the navigation was open for business, with two landing places on the Manchester side of the Irwell and a three-storey warehouse into which goods could be unloaded directly by hoist from cargo boats. This was Manchester's first purpose-built waterfront, situated at the junction of the newly constructed Water Street and Quay

Casson & Berry's Plan of Manchester and Salford, 1746 Russel Casson and John Berry published five versions of their map between 1741 and 1755. These were the first modern maps of the towns. The accompanying descriptions and illustrations emphasised not only the antiquity of the towns but also their industry, trade and wealth. Images of the Quay and the Exchange, of St Ann's Square and the grand houses of eminent citizens, plus the inset plan purporting to show Manchester in 1650, were all designed to promote an image of progress, prosperity and architectural elegance.
(Image courtesy of Chetham's Library)

Living in eighteenth-century Manchester

The last surviving early Georgian mansion in central Manchester 35–37 King Street is a five-bay brick built house, originally with wings, constructed in 1736 as a residence for Dr Peter Mainwaring (c. 1696–1785). Dr Mainwaring was a prominent Manchester citizen, physician to the Byrom family and friend of John Byrom. He was on the building committee of the Manchester Infirmary in 1753 and was a physician of the hospital from its inception until his retirement in 1778. He was made physician extraordinary in 1782 and donated many of his books to the Infirmary, forming the nucleus of the library. Outside of medicine he was a justice of the peace and an ardent Hanoverian loyalist in contrast to his Jacobite friend John Byrom. The regard in which he was held is indicated by his election as president of the Manchester Literary and Philosophical Society on its foundation in 1780. (Image © Carnegie Publishing)

Street, extending for 136 yards and built at a cost of £1,200. The Mersey and Irwell Navigation gave Manchester a water route to Liverpool. Cotton textiles destined for export were much the most important westbound cargo, while timber, raw cotton, and grain formed the bulk of the eastbound trade. It is revealing of Manchester's identity as a commercial magnet that only five years after its opening the New Quay was among the illustrations framing the 1741 edition of Casson and Berry's map. Later in the century, the building of four canals significantly extended Manchester's waterway network: the Bridgewater Canal (opened to Manchester by 1765 and most importantly to the Mersey estuary at Runcorn from 1776); the Manchester, Bolton and Bury Canal (1797); the Manchester, Ashton, Stockport and Oldham Canal (1800); and the Rochdale Canal (1804).

Also illustrated on Casson and Berry's map was the Exchange, built by Oswald Mosley in 1729 on the site of the old Conduit in Market Place (today this is the St Mary's Gate/Corporation Street corner of Marks & Spencer). This addition to Manchester's urban landscape was part of a wave of public building in English provincial towns in the early eighteenth century. Externally, Manchester's first Exchange was in the fashionable neo-classical style, but in functional arrangement it followed the more traditional pattern of a large room raised on columns above an open arcade, rather similar to many a medieval market hall. This building might well be viewed as a symbol of Manchester's burgeoning commercial status, for exchanges used by merchants for trading were often the most impressive of the new public buildings in other towns – a fine example survives today in Bristol. As monumental symbols of commerce, they were emblematic of their town's identity. However, in Manchester the first Exchange was much less significant as a trading place than its successors were to be in the nineteenth and twentieth centuries. Market Place was far too dirty and malodorous to be a suitable location for a hall of commerce. By now markets were held three times a week, on Tuesday, Thursday and Saturday, and the debris left by stallholders mired and marred the area for the rest of the week.

In 1743 the jurors of the court leet presented 'the erecting of butchers stalls within the Exchange to be a great Offence and Common Nuisance occasioned by such butchers not cleaning under their Stalls when taken down unto the great Obstruction of the Merchants and Gentlemen of the Town'. Their presentment had little effect, for ten years later their successors were complaining of the 'butchers' blocks and other Standings fixed in or near the Exchange'. But the jurors themselves had been responsible for introducing other odours to the vicinity when, in 1736, they had ordered that the fish

Byrom Street door cases Today the area west of Deansgate laid out by the Byrom family and centred on St John's Church (demolished 1931) and which includes John Street, Byrom Street and Quay Street, gives at least some idea of the appearance of the Georgian town. There are some striking 'Gothick' features such as the doorcases on Byrom Street. (Image © Carnegie Publishing)

market be moved from the Old Shambles to 'the West of the Exchange near the Great Stone Trough'.[4] It is little wonder that an alternative venue appealed to merchants, who frequented an unofficial exchange apparently located in a large room above St Ann's passage linking St Ann's Square to King Street, a more salubrious part of town. Little is known of this meeting place (although today an inscription overhead marks the presumed location).

Despite the smells emanating from the meat and fish stalls below, the 'official' Exchange was in regular use for concerts and travelling plays. George Farquhar's comedy *The Recruiting Officer* played there in 1743, and in 1750 there were performances of *Macbeth* and of *Cato*, Joseph Addison's tragedy about ancient Rome. The Exchange was also one of several meeting places for the court leet, adding to the venue's growing respectability. In due course, it came to be regarded as the town's premier place of public assembly: in 1761 some 700 'ladies and gentlemen' attended a grand ball in the upper room to celebrate the coronation of George III, and ten years later the building was used to exhibit Thomas High's version of the spinning jenny to textile manufacturers, who were impressed enough to acquire the machinery by general subscription, for the consideration of 200 guineas.[5]

Contrasts between the prosperity and living conditions of people tended to be exacerbated by economic growth: the gap between rich and poor became both larger and more visible. The wealthiest sought to live in distinct areas, exclusive to their own class and away from the lower orders. Although there had been more desirable and less desirable locations in Manchester since medieval times, the rich and the poor had often inhabited the same crowded streets, living cheek-by-jowl with each other, albeit in very different domestic circumstances. In the eighteenth century, though, the move away from the old town centre began, as the more prosperous inhabitants sought peace and quiet, space, a cleaner atmosphere, and a less congested outlook. The urban landscape was transformed and the grand brick mansions of the great merchants, as illustrated so prominently on Casson and Berry's maps, were expressions of the identity of a social class and of a wealthy merchant town, much as the picture of the Quay reflected the source of that prosperity. Buck's *Antiquities* described the Manchester of the 1720s as 'spacious, rich and populous', while a visitor forty years later, in the 1760s, saw it as 'handsome, full of good houses'.[6]

The classical proportions of these 'good houses' must have produced a sharp visual contrast with the humble timber-framed dwellings occupied by lesser citizens. Increasingly, as the more prosperous inhabitants separated

Cobden House, Quay Street A large town house of the 1770s, built by the Byrom family, later occupied by Richard Cobden in the 1830s and now the home of a legal practice. The original entrance steps and doorcase have been lost but inside it is the best preserved house of its date in the modern city centre. A notable feature is the impressive cantilevered staircase with its wrought-iron balustrade. The original owner of the house was William Allen, business partner of Edward Byrom, with whom he co-founded Manchester's first bank in 1771 (later Heywood's Bank). In 1785 Allen sold the house to William Hardman, a prosperous drysalter, who was a keen art collector. He used the house to display his collection of seventy pictures, said to include works by Titian, Canaletto and Rembrandt and to host 'gentlemen's concerts' in a specially built music room. (Image © Carnegie Publishing)

themselves from the rest, certain locations became desirable addresses. As in many other Georgian towns, squares were planned as select residential developments. St Ann's Square and its immediate vicinity (including the broad space of King Street) soon became a socially select zone, reflected in raised property values. As the better off sought social exclusivity in the town's more spacious streets and squares, they vacated the older locations. These, with their medieval and sixteenth- and seventeenth-century timber-framed properties, slipped rapidly in status. Former merchant houses were sub-divided and fell into multiple occupancy, and the poorest citizens were squeezed into the already congested back streets and alleyways of the older medieval core around the Collegiate Church and Long Millgate. This was geographical segregation by income, reflected in rental values and poor ley payments. The condition in some of these streets was soon notoriously squalid and unwholesome – as John Aikin noted at the end of the eighteenth century: 'the poor are crowded in offensive, dark, damp and incommodious habitations.'[7] In future decades many other visitors and commentators would pen similar remarks about the less salubrious neighbourhoods of Manchester.

Food riots and strikes

In 1756 the traders of Manchester petitioned the Privy Council concerning the plight 'not only of the poor but manufacturers and artisans' of the town, explaining how even in years of plenty it had relied on the importing of wheat supplies from the South and other parts of the kingdom. But 1756 and 1757 were not years of plenty – quite the opposite, for oatmeal prices were at a forty-year high. In December 1756 a public meeting opened a subscription to supply 'the industrious poor' with corn and flour and between £7,000 and £8,000 was promised. This was a period of general inflation of food prices, for the price of wheat had doubled in four years.[8] Those dependent solely or largely on manufacturing employment were hit hardest. To make matters worse, there was a downturn in trade following the outbreak of the Seven Years War with France in 1756. The result was unrest in many parts of the country and Manchester experienced serious rioting, with the worst instance of soldiers killing demonstrators before the infamous Peterloo Massacre of August 1819.

Disturbances over the price of essential foodstuffs were commonplace during years of scarcity and women were often the instigators of unrest. Following a dispute over the price of potatoes one busy market day in

John Collier (1708–1786) Collier was a satirical poet and caricaturist who wrote under the pseudonym of Tim Bobbin. Self-styled as the 'Lancashire Hogarth', he was born in Urmston, worked as a schoolmaster in Milnrow, and was buried in Rochdale parish church. Among his satirical works is a pamphlet attacking corn-engrossing after the 1757 food riot in Manchester, *Truth in a Mask: Or, Shude-Hill Fight. Being a Short Manchestrian Chronicle of the Present Times*. (Image courtesy of the Wellcome Trust, via Wikimedia Commons)

June 1757, women shoppers overturned potato sacks and bystanders eagerly pocketed the contents. Later, a crowd at Ardwick Green stopped carts bound for the market and removed the sacks of meal. Trouble was spreading rapidly. The magistrates and the 'principal inhabitants' thwarted an attempt to plunder the Meal House at the top of Market Street, but the rioters ignored admonitions from the magistrates to go back to their homes and instead attacked and looted the shop of George Bramall, a corn factor and corn chandler who with his partner Thomas Hadfield had the reputation of adulterating his flour with beans and whiting. The constables arrested two women at Bramall's shop and imprisoned them in the Dungeon. However, the crowd broke down the prison door with large forging hammers and, having thrown it into the river, carried the women prisoners off in triumph. The next day a body of colliers from out of town were repelled by force as they sought

Living in eighteenth-century Manchester

to enter Manchester and, fearing an escalation of the crisis, the Manchester merchant James Bayley, who was high sheriff of Lancashire, arrived from his country seat at Withington with an armed force hundreds strong to secure the town. However, the spectre of revolt from within caused most alarm to the authorities. According to the *Manchester Mercury*, Bayley rode on horseback, accompanied by men armed with guns, swords and clubs, and 'traversed all the principal Streets in and Avenues to the Town ... stopping in several Parts of the Town, in a very concise and elegant Manner, at each Place explained the Inconveniences that must necessarily arise to the Poor from Tumults, with proper Observations on the Dangers consequent.' The following day a large number of special constables were appointed to guard the various entry points to the town by continuous rota and this security was maintained until troops arrived a few days later.[9]

Following a poor harvest there was a second round of rioting in the winter of 1757. This time the outcome was much more serious. In November a crowd armed with clubs and sticks arrived from Ashton-under-Lyne and approached the Meal House (granary). The high sheriff, backed by a force of veteran soldiers (known as the 'Invalids'), faced them and made several arrests. The following day the crowd returned to Manchester and at a meeting with the high sheriff the leaders demanded that he give his bond that oatmeal should be sold at no more than 20 shillings a load, potatoes at 4 shillings a load and flour at five-farthings (1¼*d.*) a pound, and that these prices should be fixed for twelve months. The high sheriff replied that it was impossible to oblige the farmers to fix prices, a refusal that led to ugly scenes. He narrowly escaped death when a demonstrator lunged at him with a scythe attached to a pole. To prevent the crowd's entry to the town the soldiers withdrew to the top of Shude Hill. Here, stones and brickbats were thrown at them by a crowd now swollen by a large number of Manchester inhabitants who had been drawn to the disturbances. One of the soldiers was fatally wounded and the soldiers then sent a volley of rifle shots into the crowd, killing at least two of the rioters and a bystander on the spot. Others later died of their wounds. Most of the crowd retreated, but a group of rioters plundered a corn mill belonging to George Bramall, removing great quantities of flour and destroying the mill and the owner's house nearby. That night the crowd returned and compelled the release of a rioter who had been imprisoned in the Dungeon. The high sheriff sent an urgent request to the Secretary of War, asking for additional military force, and a troop of dragoons duly arrived to secure Manchester and the surrounding neighbourhood. The events of this day became known as the 'Shudehill Fight', after John Collier's satirical pamphlet *attacking* corn-engrossing, '*Truth in a Mask: Or, Shude-Hill Fight. Being a Short Manchestrian Chronicle of the Present Times*'. Though the 'Fight' was the most serious, it was not the only instance of soldiers killing Manchester demonstrators. In 1750, public whippings for trade infringements had led to rioting by 'insolent women' and in the fracas soldiers killed two of the crowd.[10]

Further disturbances took place in July 1762. The initial target was a Manchester dealer accused of engrossing corn (this was probably George Bramall again, as he was investigated by the court leet for this offence in the wake of the riot). A crowd of 'disorderly persons' threatened his life and when he escaped, his shop and warehouse were looted of grain, flour, beans and oatmeal. The dealer's house was the next target: all his furniture was stolen and carted off and the building hacked with pick-axes by an angry crowd which included a considerable number of women and children. Other corn dealers were similarly targeted. The town was open to the marauders and, according to the newspaper report, groups roamed the streets forcibly entering shops and private houses and demanding liquor and money. A food riot had deteriorated into looting and random violence. But the price of food remained the central issue and corn mills in the surrounding neighbourhood also became a target for the looters. Once again troops were called for, and in the meantime over thirty special constables were sworn in. Eventually the disturbances died down. The authorities sought out those men who had incited the riots, even though it took some time: two years later one of the ringleaders was arrested and sentenced to death at Lancaster for the destruction of Bramall's mill, though the sentence was commuted to 14 years' transportation.[11]

The food riot was a mechanism of popular protest in the eighteenth century. At times of scarcity, as food prices rose, it was the non-agricultural labourer who was most rapidly affected. As in Manchester, riots often involved violence against property and required the military to restore order. However, this was not unthinking mob action. Although motivated by starvation (or the fear of it), the fury that fired crowd action was fuelled by notions of a 'moral economy' and a sense of betrayal: that the governing powers had broken an unwritten contract legitimising ancient rights and customs. As we have seen from the events in Manchester, the central idea was that there was a 'just price' for food, to be asked by suppliers and market traders. Magistrates and those in authority were expected to enforce 'just' prices. The riot was an expression of frustrated anger at the failure of traditional mechanisms of influencing prices and the market trader was an easy target. However, the food riot only worked where pressure could be brought to bear on all those involved in the pricing of food, including the producers. In the manufacturing districts of Lancashire and Cheshire this was already proving impossible. The oatmeal and wheat that went to make Manchester's bread came – mostly by sea and by river – from as far afield as Wales and the south of England. With such lengthy supply lines neither crowds nor magistrates could pressurise the producers. The living standards of those in manufacturing work could be protected by other means: less by trying to influence pricing, more by pressurising employers for higher pay. Thus, from the early days of industrialisation the workers took industrial action. Often this was linked to the issue of food prices, as some employers refused to raise wages and even sought wage reductions as prices rose rapidly.

Collective action was common in the eighteenth century among a wide range of workers. They formed clubs and societies, generally masquerading under friendly society functions but often combining a collecting 'box' with the aspiration at least to protect wages and terms and conditions of employment. Wherever workers' combinations emerged from the secrecy of the clubroom they came into conflict with employers, and generally the force of the law was brought against them. Until the end of the century there was no consolidated legislation outlawing trade combinations, but there were many local Acts referring to specific trades, and the general presumption was that combinations were illegal. In Manchester and district, as elsewhere, weavers' combinations sought to regulate entry into the trade by invoking the Tudor statutes on apprenticeships (which were not formally repealed until the Combination Laws of 1799–1800). Combinations did not usually originate as attempts to defend wages, but strikes over wage rates occurred during periods of rising food prices – as in the late 1750s when disputes broke out between smallware, silk and check weavers and their employers.

The most serious dispute was a prolonged strike of check weavers in 1758, following a declaration by the employers (checkmakers) that they would prosecute all those who joined a combination. Within a short time thousands of weavers across the Manchester district were on strike. Their demands were, first, for fixed piece rates and cloth lengths with payment restored to the level that had prevailed in the 1730s. Second, they asked for recognition of their society with its charity box and the right to regulate entry to the trade. The weavers' action inspired great public sympathy, with much of the blame for the tumult being laid on the engrossers of corn. But the Royton magistrate Thomas Percival was typical when he also attacked the masters who 'took advantage of the high prices of corn to sink wages'. He condemned the sight of 'a few rich traders amongst numerous half-starved, half-cloathed poor weavers'.[12] Percival acted as arbitrator between the weavers and the master manufacturers, but negotiations, which lasted several months, eventually collapsed: the employers invoked the common law and there were several prosecutions at the Lancaster assizes. Before long the strike was over.

The success of the checkmakers in defeating their workers encouraged other groups of masters to strike at combinations in their own trades. Thus in 1759 twelve worsted smallware weavers were conveyed in carts from Manchester to the prison at Lancaster 'for combining against the manufactory'. The court dealt leniently with them, imposing small fines for the most part. Prosecutions such as these did not end industrial organisation among the weavers and, moreover, other trades began to form combinations and friendly societies, including journeymen trades such as tailors, hatters, shoemakers, masons and cabinetmakers. There were several disputes in the hatting trade in the late 1770s and early 1780s, revealing a remarkable degree of co-ordinated action across several towns including the journeymen hatters of Manchester and Stockport. These continued despite an anti-combination Act obtained by the employers in 1777. By the 1790s we first hear of the existence of combinations of cotton spinners, the early signs of industrial organisation among the embryonic cotton factory workforce.

Culture, leisure and society

By the mid-eighteenth century Manchester had become one of the regional capitals of England, the cultural as well as the economic hub of south Lancashire and north Cheshire. Following the example set by more traditional centres such as the county towns, and along with other newly arrived provincial capitals such as Liverpool and Birmingham, it developed the attributes and facilities of a centre of culture and consumption. Indeed, like other major English towns, it experienced what the historian Peter Borsay has called, an 'urban renaissance', in which cultural life was transformed in the century following 1660.

Manchester held regular assemblies from an early date, possessed thriving musical and theatrical venues, and had its own newspapers, reading rooms and coffee houses. John Byrom records in his journal that he regularly spent much time in the coffee houses of Manchester and London. Mrs Raffald's *Directory* of 1772 mentions two, the Old Coffee House and Crompton's Coffee House, both in the heart of the town close to the Exchange and Market

Place. Nearby was John Shaw's Punch House and two of the town's most popular inns, the Angel and the Bull's Head, each with a room for meetings as well as entertainments. Elizabeth Raffald's *Directory* was the first listing of Manchester businesses and is an invaluable guide to the commercial and social life of the town. But who was Elizabeth Raffald?

History rarely records the activities of women in business from this period. Major ventures would have been almost exclusively in male hands but this does not mean the complete absence of commercial endeavours run by women. The trade directories of the period, although not a complete record, reveal women engaged as independent producers, artisans, retailers and the like – in business in their own right or in partnership with male family members, usually husbands. It has been estimated from directory evidence that around 6 per cent of businesses in 1770s Manchester were

Elizabeth Raffald (1733–1781) Frontispiece from the 1782 edition of *The Experienced English Housekeeper* published in London by Baldwin. (Image in public domain, via Wikimedia Commons)

Elizabeth Raffald's Manchester Directory Frontispiece of the 1773 edition. (Image courtesy of Chetham's Library)

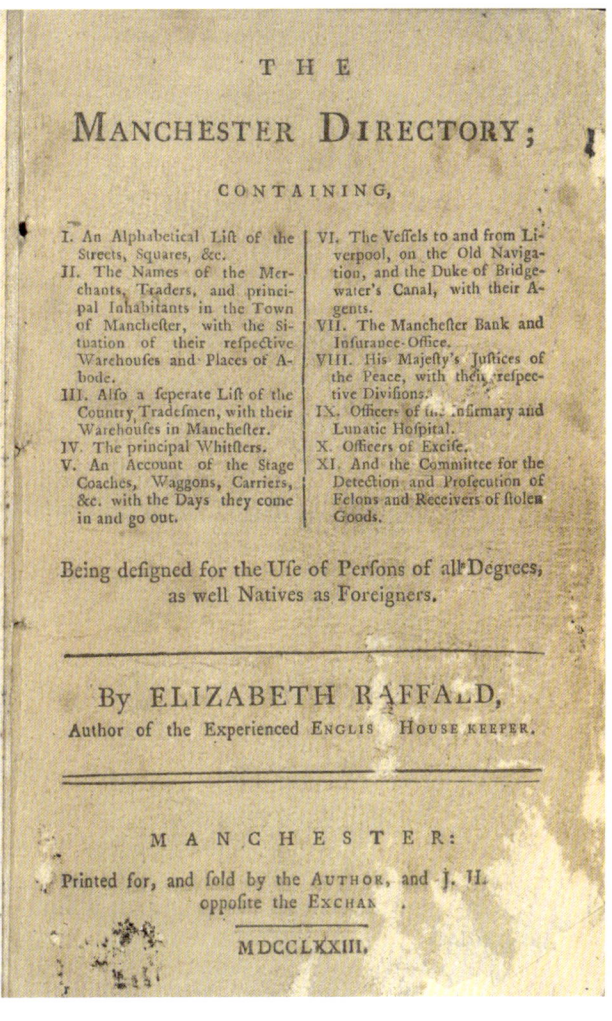

in female hands, most typically in the clothing trade, food and drink, shop keeping, and dealing.[13] Of these women the most remembered today is Elizabeth Raffald (1733–81) who appears to be have been a talented and enterprising businesswoman. She began with a shop in Fennel Street supplying 'Cold Entertainments, Hot French Dishes, Confectionaries, &c.' and in 1766 transferred her business to Exchange Alley by the Bull's Head in Market Place. This later became the Exchange Coffee House. From these premises she ran a school of cookery and domestic economy, and what was probably the first register office for servants in Manchester. She later turned her hand to the sale of cosmetics. She expanded further into catering and inn keeping and ran the King's Head in Chapel Street, Salford. The excellent cuisine and her ability to converse in French were said to have attracted many foreign visitors. She was in a competitive business. The town had inns and taverns in profusion: Raffald lists well over a hundred public houses in her *Directory*. This was not her first venture into print. Her *Experienced English Housekeeper, for the use and ease of ladies, housekeepers, cooks, &c., wrote purely from practice … consisting of near 800 original receipts* was first published in 1769. It sold well and ran to numerous editions.

Regular assemblies were a staple of the social calendar in any eighteenth-century provincial town, occasions when fashionable residents could mingle with gentry from the district. Like most other towns with a 'polite society' of attorneys, doctors, clergymen, merchants and persons of private means, Manchester acquired its own place for assemblies. This was in an upper room over St Ann's Passage linking King Street to St Ann's Square (probably the same venue as the unofficial exchange, for at this time it was common for towns to have places of accommodation for various activities). Here, balls were held weekly at a subscription of half a crown (2*s*. 6*d*.) a quarter. At the close of each assembly, 'the ladies had their maids to come with lanthorns and pattens to conduct them home'.[14] Later the upper room in the new Exchange building provided a further venue for balls, and there was an assembly room above Manchester's first theatre. Finally, a handsome and commodious purpose-built Assembly Room was provided by subscription and opened on Mosley Street in 1792.

The Exchange was an early venue for stage performances, but by the 1750s Manchester had acquired a building specifically designed for concerts and plays. The town's first theatre was located at the upper end of King Street on the former Conduit Head Field (at the corner of Marsden Street and Brown Street). What was probably a three-storey structure comprised two main rooms, one above the other: the lower was used for stage performances and the upper for dances and concerts. In 1753 the *Manchester Mercury* announced that 'at the New Theatre, the Upper End of King Street … will be performed A Grand concert of Vocal and Instrumental Music, with Concertos on the harpsichord, perform'd by the best hands, and collected from the most eminent Master. After the concert will be a Ball for the Gentlemen and Ladies.' In 1758 the same newspaper announced a performance of the masque *Acis and Galatea*.[15] In case this sounds unremittingly polite it should be remembered that plays and the theatrical profession were still far from respectable. As if to emphasise this, Elizabeth Raffald's *Directory* of 1772 tells us that the theatre also housed a tavern, the *Ram's Head*, which was probably located in the basement. Eventually, in 1775, Manchester acquired a licensed playhouse when the first Theatre Royal opened at the junction of York Street and Spring Gardens. The later venue in Peter Street was opened in 1845.

The use of subscriptions to finance musical concerts and other assemblies was an attempt to make such occasions more socially exclusive. For those who could afford to pay two shillings for one concert, or to subscribe at five shillings a quarter, there was the opportunity for a fashionable gathering. For example, in 1744 some 180 people signed up to hear works by Handel, Corelli and Germiniani. The occupations of almost half of these subscribers have been identified: 20 per cent were classed as gentry while a third were dealers of various sorts. Boyce's *Oratorio of Solomon* was performed at the Exchange in 1754 with 'several persons of Quality' in attendance. With entry determined only by price of ticket such events may have been more socially mixed than some desired, but seating was usually arranged to allow

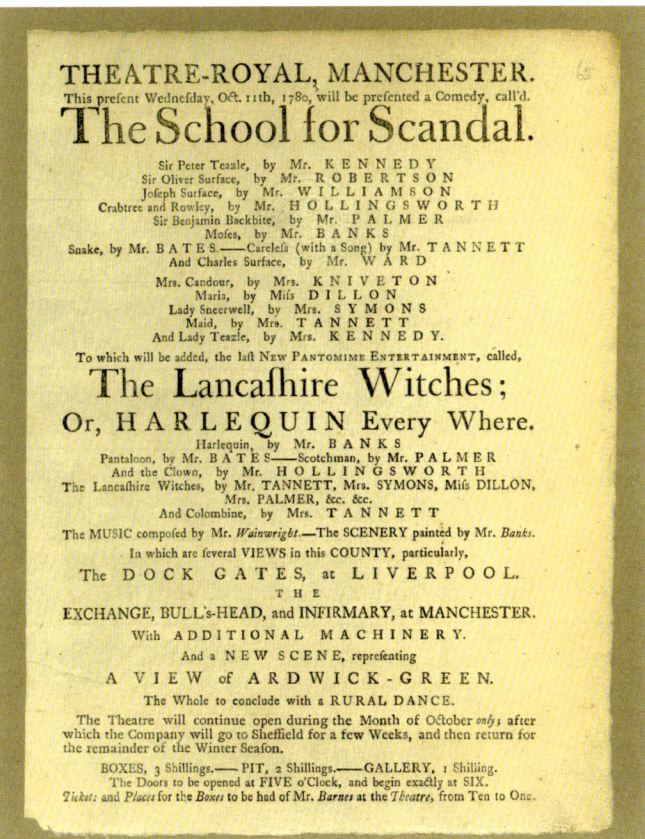

Theatre Royal playbill 1780 Richard Brinsley Sheridan's celebrated comedy of manners *The School for Scandal* was first performed at the Drury Lane Theatre, London, in 1777. Its performance in Manchester was accompanied by a curious 'pantomime' combining characters from the Italian Commedia dell'arte and the Lancashire witches of Pendle Hill against the backdrop of a series of local scenes clearly aimed at enhancing audience numbers. (Image courtesy of Chetham's Library)

the 'genteel' to be separate from the rest, and they could also indulge in conspicuous consumption by the purchase of the accompanying programme, which alone could cost a princely three shillings.[16]

The most distinctive and significant social institutions of Georgian England were its associations, societies and clubs. These expressed many different varieties of sociability: political, religious, charitable, learned, social and sporting. In Manchester they ranged from politically partisan drinking and social clubs such as John Shaw's (which was Tory and Anglican) to the Agricultural Society founded in 1767. Manchester had one of the earliest mathematical societies, although its most important learned societies were founded after 1780.

The most significant product of association in eighteenth-century Manchester was the Infirmary. Founded in 1752, this charitable institution enjoyed support across party and sectarian divides, and went some way towards healing the split among the town's 'principal inhabitants' following the 1745 rebellion (see below). Previously public benevolence had been channelled through the Church or charities established by bequest, but the eighteenth century saw the voluntary society emerge as the principal philanthropic mechanism. Infirmaries, pre-eminent among such causes, were founded in many towns from the mid-century onwards. Funded by subscription and self-governing in character, these voluntary hospitals became the jewels of civic philanthropy. Moreover, the idea became established that charity and the liberal arts were intimately linked because each was seen to promote moral improvement in the donors and the recipients. Music seems to have been the preferred vehicle for philanthropy and in Manchester this found reflection in concerts in aid of the Infirmary. These were held fortnightly in the 1750s: over £60 was raised by one such concert in 1758 by a 'crowded and genteel audience'.

In the eighteenth century there was an active and varied popular culture of sports and festivities, with some activities and events that crossed class lines. Edward Byrom observed in a pamphlet of 1733 that all social orders engaged in 'Box and Dice, Cards, Cocks and Race Horses'. Horse-race meetings were a regular feature of Manchester's sporting calendar. There is record of horse racing at Kersal Moor as early as 1687 and by the 1730s this became the venue for Manchester's annual horse races which, with a short break in the middle of the century, remained here until the Castle Irwell racecourse was opened in nearby Lower Broughton in the 1840s. Races also took place at other venues. A broadside of 1709, advertising a race in Horrock's Field, Manchester, promised that for four guineas 'those Gentlemen, Sportsmen,

Infirmary, Dispensary and Lunatic Asylum Initially housed in Garden Street, Shudehill, the Infirmary relocated in 1755 to its grand, purpose-built premises at Piccadilly on land leased from Sir Oswald Mosley. The large ornamental pond replaced the daube holes shown on Casson and Berry's map which had provided the town with building clay for centuries. Image from *Lancashire Illustrated*, 1831. (Image courtesy of the Wellcome Trust, via Wikimedia Commons)

etc. who please to attend, may depend on a meeting with excellent Sport, and plenty of hard Cash, on the Occasion'. Race meetings were lively and varied social gatherings frequented by all social classes, although the wealthy endeavoured to maintain the barriers of social distinction by attending the evening balls and assemblies that inevitably accompanied meets. Cockfighting was an ancient sport and in Manchester as early as 1587 the court leet records mention a cockpit or 'cockfightplace', probably located in Cockpit Hill (a narrow thoroughfare running from Market Place to Market Street Lane). By the eighteenth century there were other venues, and cocking was a professionally organised business. In 1762 the *Manchester Mercury* announced the sale of a cockpit 'situate at the Top of Deansgate' and comprising 'upwards of 200 pens, two good feeding Rooms and Rooms for laying of Straw'. The premises came replete with a 'Bowling Green' and 'a good accustom'd Public House'. Whatever the commercial fortunes of this venture, there were frequent advertisements in the local press for cockfights and, as well as that on Deansgate, other cockpits continued to operate. Like horse races,

Market Place looking to Market Street Market Place was the heart of Manchester from medieval times through to the early nineteenth century when this print was published. The semi-circular building on the right is the second Manchester Exchange, erected in 1809. Ahead is Market Street as it looked before it was widened and redeveloped in the 1820s. John Ralston, *Views of the Ancient Buildings of Manchester*, 1823. (Image courtesy of Chetham's Library)

cockfights were occasions for gambling, a predilection that recognises no social distinction.

Such sports were a traditional element in a culture that transcended social class. However, the eighteenth century witnessed the emergence of a more self-consciously rational and literate culture, its chief expression being the rise of a newspaper press. Manchester witnessed at least 17 attempts to start a newspaper or periodical during the century to 1780. The earliest Manchester paper, published in 1719 by Roger Adams, was short-lived but by the 1730s a regular weekly press had emerged. Robert Whitworth's *Manchester Magazine* (which began as the *Manchester Gazette* but underwent several title changes) ran from 1737 to 1760. This was the only newspaper regularly published in the town until in 1752 Joseph Harrop founded the *Manchester Mercury*, which became the chief Manchester newspaper until it ceased publication in 1830. In its columns the emphasis on trade and the regular advertisements for property auctions and sales of expensive goods suggest it was aimed at a 'middling sorts' readership. Weekly provincial papers mainly filled their few pages with a digest of the London press and a lot of advertising, and offered only the tiniest smattering of local news. Much local information was still conveyed by the bellman (or town crier), who would ring his bell and shout out the news from various vantage points. There are numerous instances of the court leet jurors employing the bellman to convey market news, although by 1766 they were also advertising the same in the *Manchester Mercury*.[17]

There was a thirst for news and it seems that what the newspaper reader wanted most was commercial intelligence – news of dividends, bankruptcies, shipping movements, wars and uprisings … in short, anything that might have a bearing on trade.

The *Manchester Mercury* cost 1½d. and was published on Tuesday, the town's main market day. Some idea of the pace of news can be obtained from the story that Harrop's paper outsold Whitworth's *Manchester Magazine* because of his arrangement to obtain Saturday's *London Gazette* early. He would meet the night mail at Derby and get the latest edition of the London paper to Manchester by Monday afternoon, enabling him to publish all the latest London and foreign news on the following day. Many readers consulted the papers in coffee houses and inns (where it was customary to read aloud to others) or in reading rooms such as John Berry's Long Room, where local and London newspapers were available to subscribers who paid two shillings a quarter; others could gain entry at a penny a time. The *Manchester Mercury* enjoyed a readership in surrounding towns and villages in Lancashire, Cheshire and Yorkshire, some only accessible by packhorse track. To reach his geographically dispersed customers Harrop employed agents to sell the papers, accept advertisements and collect subscriptions. In 1755 the paper claimed a circulation of 2,000. The real readership must have been much higher: historians estimate that in the eighteenth century between 20 and 30 people would read each copy of a newspaper.

Whitworth and Harrop were also printers and book publishers. The former published the first edition of the works of the dialect

The first book to be printed in Manchester This was published by Roger Adams in 1719 and dedicated to 'the Vertuous and Religious Lady Bland'. (Image courtesy of Chetham's Library)

poet and writer Tim Bobbin, although Joseph Harrop's list was much longer, with numerous books, tracts, sermons and playbills. Among his most famous publications are the large paper copies of Byrom's *Miscellaneous Poems* and Mrs Raffald's *Experienced English Housekeeper*. The quality of his printing was high, often decorated with elaborate woodcuts. However, like Whitworth and other provincial printers of their era, he was dependent on other sources of income, operating as a bookseller and stationer and even acting as an agent for the sale of nostrums or patent medicines. The first book to be printed in Manchester was John Jackson's *Mathematical Lectures Read to the Mathematical Society at Manchester*, published by Roger Adams in 1719. Books had to be sold, and the eighteenth century saw new centres of the country book trade in the manufacturing towns of Leeds, Birmingham and Manchester with several new and second-hand book dealers many of whom, like the wigmaker and barber Edmund Harrold, combined the buying and selling of books with other trades.[18]

Politics, religion and authority

In the eyes of the nation the only challenge to Manchester's ubiquitous label as a trading town was its identification with religious faction and political dispute. Religion and politics were intertwined in the eighteenth century. Political parties (Whig and Tory) had formed in the parliaments of the late seventeenth century and soon found an echo in the local politics of the provinces. Religious differences and divisions hardened as the sectarian divides of the civil war era were complicated further by fractures within Protestantism. The chief division was between those who conformed to the doctrines and practices of the Established Church of England and those who dissented (the nonconformists or dissenters). Within Anglicanism itself divisions emerged between what can broadly be described as the High Church and the Low Church, with different congregations coalescing around each faction. Added to this were the tensions created by the association of Roman Catholicism with treason, which had endured since the Reformation in the sixteenth century and was made more acute by the events of 1688–89. The ascendancy of the firmly Protestant House of Hanover in 1714 effectively denied the throne to the Stuart dynasty, whose Catholic faith tainted the support given by some Tories for their cause – especially since for much of the century England was involved a succession of wars with Catholic France. The failed military campaigns of the 'Pretenders' in 1715 and 1745 further emphasised the exclusion of the Stuarts and deprived the Tories of national political power, which remained in the hands of the Whigs for much of the first half of the eighteenth century. The role of Manchester in these national events was to have implications for the town's reputation. It was the only place in England to raise a regiment of soldiers (the so-called 'Manchester Regiment') to fight in support of the Pretender in 1745 and for its pains was subject to military occupation for eighteen months in 1745–46.

Local loyalties lay along political and religious fault lines. A satirical pamphlet by Thomas Percival, published in 1748, described the meeting in a Manchester coffee house of one 'Mr Whig-love' with a certain 'Mr Trew-blew'. Their violent verbal exchanges frightened off 'Mr Tradelove', a moderate man of commerce.[19] Percival was a Presbyterian and worshipped at the Cross Street chapel. This had been founded in 1694, after the Toleration Act of 1689 had granted limited rights of religious freedom to Protestant dissenters. In the eyes of Jacobite-leaning Tories the Presbyterians were linked with the regicide of Charles I and were therefore seen as dangerous republicans. The Presbyterians were always a small minority in the town, although the congregation at the dissenters' meeting house on Cross Street include several wealthy and influential worshippers. Within the Established Church, 'High Churchmen' prized the exclusive authority of the Church of England, its bishops and the Anglican liturgy and 'Low Churchmen', though conforming to official Church of England practices, allowed greater toleration on matters of doctrine, liturgical practice, and ecclesiastical organisation.

In Manchester the division was between the Collegiate Church and St Ann's church. The lady of the manor, Ann Bland, née Mosley, may have founded the latter as a counter-balance to the views, both religious and political, prevalent at the Collegiate Church. Although some individuals attended services at both churches, the congregation at St Ann's was more likely to be Low Church in religion and Whig in politics while the Collegiate Church was

Jacobites in Manchester 1745 A blue plaque marks the site in Artillery Street used by the Jacobite forces of Charles Edward Stuart in 1745. (Image © Carnegie Publishing)

Living in eighteenth-century Manchester

definitely High Church and Tory. The latter group had the upper hand in the town's affairs. Throughout the eighteenth century Tory High Churchmen enjoyed the lion's share of local power as churchwardens and sidesmen of the Collegiate Church, as officers of the court leet, and as magistrates. It was the strength of High Church Tories in the town that gave credence to Manchester's reputation as anti-Hanoverian and pro-Stuart. The Collegiate Church itself acquired the reputation of being a Jacobite enclave. Religious divisions had hardened after 1660 and ran deep in the town. What is surprising is that Manchester, which had been parliamentarian and Puritan in the Civil War, became linked in the national consciousness with a totally contrary world view.

During the first half of the eighteenth century there were recurrent threats of invasion and insurrection on behalf of the Stuart claimants to the throne. The chief of these were the so-called '15 and '45. In 1715 a major rising in support of James Edward Stuart (the 'Old Pretender', or James III to his supporters) originated in Scotland, stimulated among other factors by hostility to the 1707 Act of Union with England, which had created the new United Kingdom of Great Britain. The rebellion spread into northern England and was finally defeated at the Battle of Preston (the 'Preston Fight'). In 1745 the most serious attempt at invasion, led personally by Charles Edward Stuart ('Bonnie Prince Charlie', or the 'Young Pretender') came within 120 miles of London before retreating north, ultimately to face annihilation at the bloody Battle of Culloden. Manchester played a significant part in the events of both the '15 and the '45. The accession to the throne of George I in 1714 had confirmed the Whig ascendancy in national politics and the thwarting of Tory ambitions. The events of the following year reflect a mixture of frustration and hope among those Tories who (oddly, we might think) saw the Catholic Stuarts as the best chance of protecting the Church of England from the spectre of Presbyterianism. They hankered after the kind of conservative Protestant religious settlement they believed had prevailed before the Civil War under the early Stuart monarchs.

In the summer of 1715, prior to the Jacobite rising in Scotland, there was a series of riotous attacks on dissenters' meeting houses in the West Midlands and Lancashire. The most serious violence occurred in Manchester. The meeting house on Cross Street was systematically destroyed, almost brick by brick, over several days of rioting during June and July. A crowd of some 300–400 smashed the windows, pulled the slates from the roof, and partly demolished the walls. A few days later they sacked the interior and burned the pulpit and pews, finally returning to complete the destruction of the building, which was described as 'flattened'. There is evidence that some local High Church Tories orchestrated the riots, although the rioters themselves mostly had plebeian occupations. The mob attacked other meeting houses in the neighbourhood. Alarm about the events spread to government ministers and even the king. A troop of dragoons was despatched to the town to restore order. The rioters may not all have been Jacobites, but Presbyterian chapels were the targets and there were reported cries of 'Down with the Rump' (the name given the purged House of Commons that had ordered the trial of Charles I for treason in 1649).[20] Among those arrested for the riot in Manchester was Thomas Syddall, a local blacksmith, described as the 'colonel of the mob'. He was tried and imprisoned in Lancaster Castle but was later freed by the Scottish Jacobite army and joined the rebels, only to be captured soon after at the 'Preston Fight'. For this latter treasonous act, rather than for his part in the riot at Manchester, he was executed. However, the execution took place locally, at Knott Mill, and his severed head was placed on a spike in front of the Exchange, facing towards the very Presbyterian chapel he had destroyed.

The Manchester Tories were tarnished by the links with Jacobitism in 1715 but they continued to exercise an influence in the town, which they were determined to maintain. This was thrown into sharp relief by a dispute in 1729 over the funding of a new workhouse. Subscriptions were raised and trustees appointed from High Church, Low Church and dissenting factions. Despite the fact that £2,000 was donated towards the venture the High Church Tories withdrew their support, fearing that Low Church Whigs and Presbyterian Whigs together would outnumber them. In the aftermath the faction fighting persisted as all the parties to the dispute continued to exchange vitriolic abuse.

These divisions were exposed once more with the dramatic events of 1745, which also revealed the limits of local support for the Jacobite cause. The only real chance the Jacobites had of victory was if they were to enjoy substantial military support from a foreign power. Despite repeated wars with the French, this never materialised on the necessary scale. The military adventures of 1745 arose because Charles Edward Stuart, frustrated at French unwillingness to invade, decided to finance his own rising. He garnered a surprising level of support in the Highlands, encouraging his Jacobite army to move into lowland Scotland, winning a victory at Prestonpans and occupying Edinburgh for two months. The success of the rebels held as they marched into England during November 1745, avoiding the loyal force under General George Wade who had gathered at Newcastle and instead attacking Carlisle, which surrendered after a siege of two days. Wade's force marched from Newcastle but arrived too late. The fall of Carlisle yielded the Highland army, of around 6,000 men, a significant cache of arms and horses. Thus

Charles Edward Stuart c. 1745 A portrait, painted around the time of the Jacobite Rising by Scottish artist, Allan Ramsay. (Image courtesy of National Galleries of Scotland, via Wikimedia Commons)

strengthened militarily and emboldened by victory, they took the road south.

As the Young Pretender's army approached Manchester, a subscription fund of almost £2,000 was raised to pay for a loyalist force to resist him. Prominent Presbyterians and Low Church Whigs as well as some High Church Tories were among the subscribers. However, this militia, which was led by the lord lieutenant of the county, Lord Derby, strategically withdrew as the Pretender's forces approached, leaving Manchester open to the rebel advance. Several wealthy Whigs and their families left town, taking their valuables with them on carts. They included Robert Whitworth, publisher of the *Manchester Magazine*. In his absence, his press was commandeered for the printing of Jacobite propaganda. On 28 November the Pretender's emissary reached the town and immediately began to invite recruits. Despite a hostile reception from some, sufficient supporters were obtained to secure his safety until the first of the rebels arrived around 3 p.m. According to the celebrated Manchester diarist John Byrom, it took only 'two men in highland dress and a woman with a drum on her knee' to take the town. The whole force reached Manchester the following day, the prince himself riding in during the afternoon. His father was declared 'James III' by proclamation from the Market Cross. The house of the wealthy linen draper John Dickinson, in Market Street, was chosen as the prince's headquarters and was for this reason known in later years as 'The Palace'.

The rebels hoped that Manchester, with its Jacobite sympathisers in the Collegiate Church, would support their cause. On the night of the prince's arrival Jacobite supporters were prominent. Houses were illuminated, bonfires lit, and bells rung. John Clayton, one of the chaplains at the Collegiate Church, reputedly knelt in public before the Pretender and prayed for his success. The non-juring bishop and Jacobite adherent, Thomas Deacon, who ministered to a small congregation in the town, gave three of his sons to join the Jacobite forces. The rebels attempted to drum up broader support and some three hundred recruits formed what became known as 'The Manchester Regiment' under the leadership of the Burnley recusant, Francis Towneley. This was the only place in England to give the Pretender more than ten new recruits. It was a heterogeneous and geographically diverse assembly. Apart from a number of Catholic and convinced Jacobite volunteers, the majority were drawn from rural occupations, village craftsmen and farmworkers. But the best-represented occupation was weaving. Many of the recruits were dissatisfied apprentices, some newly arrived in Manchester and without work. The majority were under 24, one as young as twelve. They each received a shilling and were fed and billeted. Many, faced with poverty or trapped by apprenticeships, must have seen joining the Stuart army as a means of escape. While the officers and sergeants were from the Manchester area, the men came from a variety of other locations – chiefly from in and around Wigan and Preston, both areas with large Catholic populations.

The rebel army marched south after three days, reaching Derby on 2 December, but after several days' deliberation retreated north again. Faced with the prospect of encountering substantial British armies between them and London, and in the absence of any popular pro-Jacobite uprising, they returned to Manchester in retreat on 9 December. This time the populace was openly hostile. Clods of mud assailed them as they dragged their feet through the town. When the prince arrived a contribution of £5,000 was demanded from the constables but only £2,500 was collected, and he and his forces left the town next day. The Manchester Regiment experienced a huge desertion rate and was little over a hundred strong when the prince entrusted it with the defence of Carlisle, which surrendered at the end of the month. The news of the capture of Carlisle and the later victory of Culloden were the occasion for celebrations in Manchester as elsewhere, and this time the bonfires and bell ringing were in a different cause.

The officers of the Manchester Regiment were tried for high treason in July 1746, and some were executed at Kennington near London. The heads of Lieutenant Thomas Deacon (the son of the non-juring bishop) and the adjutant Thomas Syddall, whose father had been executed in the rising of 1715, were sent up to Manchester, and fixed on poles on the Exchange. They remained on view in this prominent position in Market Place for five years before being stolen. The men of the regiment were tried at Carlisle in August and September 1746, and many were executed. Several Manchester families from all social ranks had relatives on trial for treason, and many suffered the death penalty. Although there were ample displays of allegiance to the Hanoverian regime, the loyalty of Manchester had been made suspect by the events of 1745 and the town was put under martial law for eighteenth months. The atmosphere in Manchester was ugly. The mob, emboldened by the presence of the soldiery, displayed marked hostility towards any hint of Jacobitism. In October 1746 a national day of thanksgiving for the suppression of the rebellion was observed in Manchester by attacks on the homes of prominent Jacobites led by groups of soldiers. The houses of Thomas Deacon's father and of the widow of Thomas Syddall were particular targets.[21]

After the failure of the '45 the potential for a Stuart restoration seemed impossibly remote, but in Manchester tensions remained high for the rest of the decade. John Byrom's journal reveals that in the late 1740s animosities repeatedly infected polite social occasions such as assemblies and balls, when 'Jacobite' sympathisers like Byrom took part in dances with deliberately provocative names like 'Down with the Rump' and blows were subsequently exchanged. However, despite persistent partisan rivalries tensions did gradually decline. This is apparent in the cross-party support for the Infirmary in 1752, 'happily founded on a Principle, in which worthy and honest Persons of all Religions and all Parties, Unite'.[22] This was a clear and deliberate move to eradicate division through consensus and collaboration. Moreover, from the 1750s onwards there were repeated displays of patriotic loyalty that united most in the town. Imperial triumphs, such as Wolfe's victory at Quebec, were celebrated, and moments of national celebration observed, such as the coronation of George III. Indeed in 1775 the gentlemen, clergy, manufacturers and inhabitants of Manchester submitted the very first loyal address to the king pledging support for the war against the American colonies.[23] The days of the '15 and the '45 were long forgotten and Manchester had successfully reinvented itself as a town noted for its tireless pursuit of trade and its conspicuous displays of patriotism and loyalty to the Crown.

Manchester in 1780

By the second half of the eighteenth century, Manchester had become a provincial centre of the very first rank, already attracting fascinated interest for its urban growth, commercial life and transport innovations. Roads, packhorse routes and canals converged on Manchester markets. As well as the Irwell and Mersey Navigation, by the 1780s its canal system included the Bridgewater Canal, which John Aikin observed in 1795 had 'rendered the name of the Duke of Bridgewater so celebrated in the history of canal-navigation'.[24] This, the world's first industrial canal, was constructed to transport coals to Manchester from the duke's mines at Worsley and

John Byrom (1692–1763) The youngest son of Edward Byrom, a prosperous Manchester linen draper. Wealth accruing from trade enabled John Byrom, to be educated at Cambridge University, where he was elected a fellow of Trinity College in 1714. There he began writing poetry and invented a system of shorthand, which he afterwards taught. Most remembered today as the author of the words to the hymn 'Christians Awake', Byrom was elected a fellow of the Royal Society in 1724 and his diaries provide interesting portraits and letters of the many great men of his time whom he knew intimately. He was a Jacobite sympathiser and an acute observer of the politics and society of his home town of Manchester. (Image courtesy of the Wellcome Trust, via Wikimedia Commons)

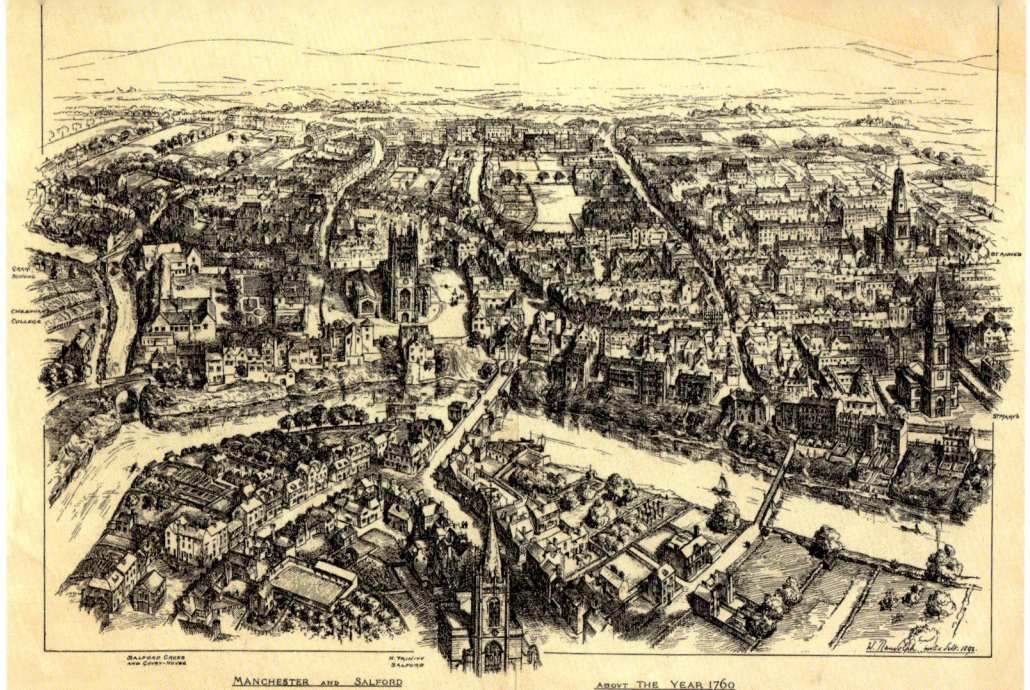

Manchester in 1760 This artist's impression shows the River Irwell and the Collegiate Church in the foreground with the narrowness of Market Street rising from the bustle of Market Place to open fields at what is now Piccadilly on the outskirts of town.
(Image © Manchester Libraries, Information and Archives)

culminated in an extensive canal basin at Castlefield on the western edge of the town. Urban growth proceeded apace and was to accelerate, with the town's population tripling in the last quarter of the century. In 1783 James Ogden observed that, 'The large and populous town of Manchester has now excited the attention and curiosity of strangers, on account of its extensive trade and the rapid increase of its buildings, with the enlargement of its streets'.[25] Manchester was a boom town, before a single cotton spinning mill had been built.

With the benefit of hindsight we can see that the nineteenth-century pre-eminence of Manchester was rooted in conditions, decisions and a measure of good luck that had been inherited from the previous century and which can even be traced back to the years around 1600. By the 1780s the town was already the hub of an extensive trading network and the vital force in a manufacturing system which combined rural and urban production. Manchester goods, and the Manchester men who marketed them, had generated a positive brand known across the land. The town had developed what we would now recognise as a business mentality. Moreover, the supreme stroke of good fortune was the worldwide export potential of cotton, the very product that Manchester was to make its own. Technological innovations in cotton spinning underpinned the phenomenon and the revolution was already under way when steam-powered production arrived to accelerate the process greatly. The previous century had served to secure Manchester a place on the national platform, but the events of the seventy years between 1780 and 1850 were to push it firmly onto the world stage, as Manchester emerged as the first industrial city and a global symbol of the urban industrial revolution.

Tinker's Plan of Manchester and Salford, 1772 Thomas Tinker was a surveyor living in Salford. His plan, based on a survey of 1772, focuses on the principal streets and is the only known map of the town between Casson & Berry's mid-century plans and the maps completed in the 1790s by William Green and Charles Laurent. Comparison with Casson & Berry's 1746 map reveals new streets, notably along Deansgate and the new churches of St Mary (1756), St Paul (1765) and St John (1768). Oldham Street, which in 1772 was in the process of being adopted as a new public thoroughfare, is named as 'The Intended Street'. The Infirmary buildings can be seen at what later becomes Piccadilly but Mosley Street and Portland Street were yet to be laid out. This is a snapshot of Manchester before the massive urban development that was to take place over the next fifty years – its population multiplied over five and a half times by 1821 and Manchester became the most important centre of the urban industrial revolution. Although Tinker's is not as comprehensive as the maps to be published in the 1790s, it is a reasonable portrait of a town that had grown over the previous century but was still a place of pedestrian scale in which all parts were within walking distance and the countryside was never far away
(Image © Manchester Libraries, Information and Archives)

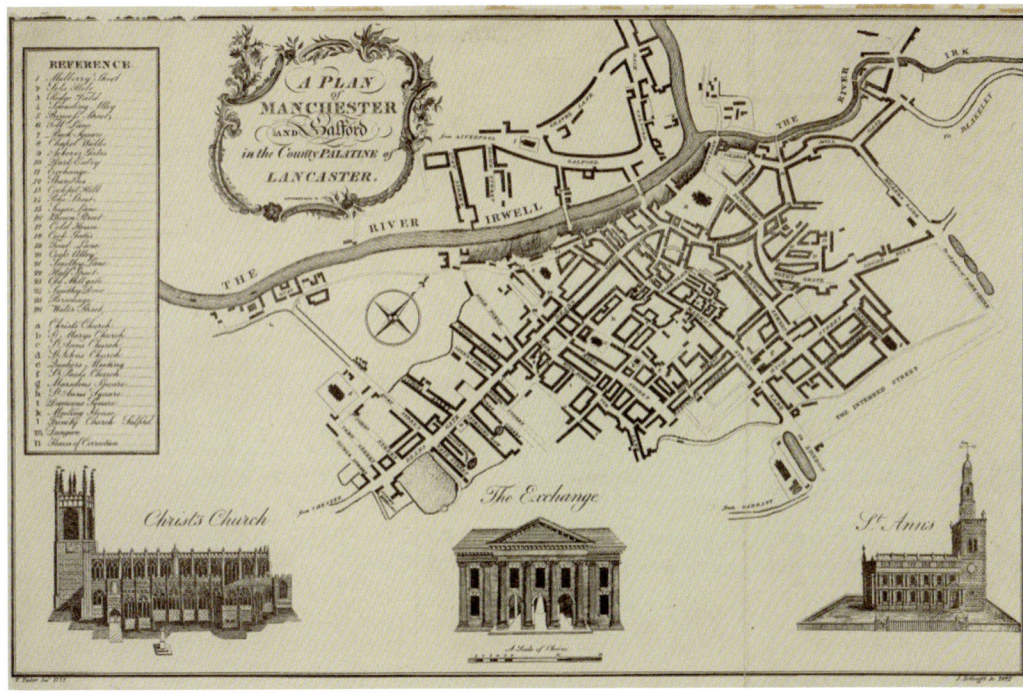

Living in eighteenth-century Manchester

Notes and references

Preface

1. For an assessment of the historical relationship between Manchester and Salford see John Garrard & Alan Kidd, '"Too near neighbours to be good friends": Manchester and Salford' in J. Garrard & E. Mikhailova, eds., *Twin Cities: Urban Communities, Borders and Relationships Over Time* (Routledge, 2019), pp.37–50.

Chapter 1: Mamucium: a Roman fort

1. For a discussion of the evidence see John Hind, 'The Roman name for Manchester' in G.D.B. Jones *et al.*, (ed S. Grealey) *Roman Manchester* (Manchester, 1974).
2. For a survey of the history of discovery and excavation see Shelagh Grealey, 'Roman Manchester: exploration, 1540–1972' in Jones, *Roman Manchester*; M. Nevell, *Manchester: The Hidden History* (Stroud, 2008), ch. 2.
3. S. Bryant *et al.*, *The Archaeological History of Greater Manchester, Vol. III, Roman Manchester: A Frontier Settlement* (Greater Manchester Archaeological Unit: Manchester, 1986), pp. 131–40.
4. There is some evidence of pre-Roman trade in the vicinity, while a few early non-Roman Mediterranean coins and Iron Age issues from other parts of Britain indicate that there were trading links between the Mediterranean and the North West around the time of the Roman arrival. See K.J. Matthews, 'The Iron Age of north-west England: a socio-economic model', *Journal of the Chester Archaeological Society* (2002), pp. 1–51; F.A. Bruton, *The Roman Fort at Manchester* (1909).
5. See P. Bidwell, *Roman Forts in Britain* (Batsford/English Heritage, 1997), ch. 6.
6. For Roman building types in Manchester see Norman Redhead, 'The Archaeology of South-East Lancashire' in C. Hartwell, M. Hyde & N. Pevsner, *The Buildings of England, Lancashire: Manchester and the South-East* (Yale University Press, 2004), pp. 16–17.
7. See Jones, *Roman Manchester*.
8. A list of possible Roman objects found in the Castlefield area, with a map to show the precise location of each find over the years, is included in Bryant, *Archaeological History of Greater Manchester, Vol. III*, pp. 2-3. See also Nevell, *Manchester: The Hidden History*, ch. 2.
9. Bruton, *Roman Fort*, pp. 34ff; Jones, *Roman Manchester*, p. 16.
10. G.D.B. Jones and P. Reynolds, *The Deansgate Excavations* (Greater Manchester Council, 1978), pp. 15–16; D. Shotter, *Romans and Britons in North West England* (Centre for North West Regional Studies, 2004), p. 73.

Chapter 2: Mamecestre: a medieval market town

1. M. Morris (ed.), *Medieval Manchester: A Regional Study*, The Archaeology of Greater Manchester vol. I (1983), p. 15.
2. Morris (ed.), *Medieval Manchester*, pp. 9–12.
3. D. Griffiths, 'The North-West frontier' in N. Higham and D.H. Hills (eds), *Edward the Elder* (London: Routledge, 2001), pp. 167–87. Morris (ed.), *Medieval Manchester*, pp. 9–12; M. Nevell, *Manchester: The Hidden History* (Stroud, 2008), pp. 36–7.
4. J. Tait, *Mediaeval Manchester and the Origins of Lancashire* (Manchester, 1904), pp. 23–4.
5. Morris (ed.), *Medieval Manchester*, ch. 5.
6. M. de Wolf Hemmeon, *Burgage Tenure In Mediaeval England* (2004), pp. 22–3.
7. J. Tait, *The Medieval English Borough: Studies on its origins and constitutional history* (Manchester, 1968), p. 205.

8 See map on page 20 of Morris (ed.), *Medieval Manchester*. Evidence for the date of the Manchester fulling mill is in W. Farrer (ed.), *Lancashire inquests, extents and feudal aids*, Record Society of Lancashire and Cheshire Manchester (1903).

9 E.M. Carus-Wilson, 'An industrial revolution of the thirteenth century', *Economic History Review*, 11 (1941), 50–1, 59.

10 Morris (ed.), *Medieval Manchester*, p. 35, Nevell, *Manchester: The Hidden History*, p. 44.

11 G. Timmins, *Made in Lancashire: A study of regional industrialisation*, ch. 1; R.S. Schofield, 'The geographical distribution of wealth in England, 1334–1649', *Economic History Review*, 2nd ser., 18 (1965), pp. 483–510, esp. pp. 503–9; E.J. Buckatzsch, 'The geographical distribution of wealth in England, 1086–1843, *Economic History Review*, 2nd ser., 3 (1950–51), pp. 180–202.

Chapter 3: 'The fairest, best builded, quikkest and most populous tounne of al Lancastreshire': Manchester 1543–1660

1 Calculated from the table in C. Horner (ed.), *Early Modern Manchester* (Manchester Region History Review, 2008), essay by A.G. Crosby, p. 3. See also T. Arkell 'Identifying regional variations from the hearth tax', *Local Historian*, 33 (2003), 148–74.

2 E.A. Wrigley and R.S. Schofield, *The Population History of England, 1541–1871* (Cambridge, 1989) pp. 531–3; C.B. Phillips and J.H. Smith, *Lancashire and Cheshire from AD 1540* (Routledge, 1994), p. 6; Nevell, *Manchester: The Hidden History*, pp. 63–5.

3 See N. Lowe, *The Lancashire Textile Industry in the Sixteenth Century*, Chetham Society (1972), pp. 3–5.

4 T.S. Willan, *Elizabethan Manchester*, Chetham Society (1980), pp. 124–5.

5 For interesting evidence see the analysis of tax assessments, especially the lay subsidy returns of 1334 and 1524–25 in Morris (ed.), *Medieval Manchester*, pp.23–5, and figure 13. This follows, among others, the unpublished work of J. Sheail, 'The regional distribution of wealth in England as indicated in the lay subsidy returns, 1524–25', Ph.D. thesis, University of London (1965).

6 For the inventory see Lowe, *Lancashire Textile Industry*, pp. 106–12 and discussion on pp. 31–3.

7 T.S. Willan, 'Manchester clothiers in the early seventeenth century', *Textile History*, 10 (1979), pp. 175–83.

8 A.P. Wadsworth and J. De Lacy Mann, *The Cotton Trade and Industrial Lancashire, 1600–1780* (Manchester University Press, 1931), p. 21. N.B. Harte, *The New Draperies in the Low Countries and England* (Oxford, 1997).

9 S.J. Guscott, *Humphrey Chetham, 1580–1653: Fortune, Politics and Mercantile Culture in Seventeenth-Century England*, Chetham Society (2003), ch. 1. Entry on Humphrey Chetham by A.G. Crosby, *Oxford Dictionary of National Biography*, http://www.oxforddnb.com/

10 *Court Leet Records of the Manor of Manchester* (herafter *CLR*), vol. II, pp. 292–3.

11 *CLR*, vol. I, p. 161.

12 *CLR*, vol. III, p. 8.

13 *CLR*, vol. I, p. 224.

14 *CLR*, vol. I, p. 259.

15 W.K. Jordan, *The Social Institutions of Lancashire, 1480-1660*, Chetham Society (1962), pp. 21, 117, 119. See ibid., p. v for the other counties in the survey.

16 Jordan, *Social Institutions*, pp. 18-19.

17 *CLR*, vol. II, p. 178.

18 *CLR*, vol. III, p. 165.

19 For the Bowker family and contrasting death rates see Marnie Mason, 'Manchester in 1645: the effects and social consequences of Plague', *Transactions of the Lancashire & Cheshire Antiquarian Society*, 94 (1998), esp. pp. 5, 19–20. For the estimates of the total death toll see T.S. Willan, 'Plague in perspective: the case of Manchester in 1605', *Transactions of the Historic Society of Lancashire & Cheshire*, 132 (1982), 29–40.

20 B.G. Blackwood, *The Lancashire Gentry and the Great Rebellion*, Chetham Society (1978), pp. 63, 65.

21 Blackwood, *Lancashire Gentry and the Great Rebellion*; E. Broxap, *The Great Civil War in Lancashire, 1642–1651* (Manchester, 1973); N. Dore, *The Great Civil War in the Manchester Area* (Manchester, 1972); J.M. Gratton, *The Parliamentarian and Royalist War Effort in Lancashire, 1642–1651*, Chetham Society (2010), esp. pp. 178–9, 246–7.

22 Quoted in Margaret James, *Social Problems and Policy During the Puritan Revolution* (1930), p. 244.

23 For the basis of such calculations based on mean household size see P. Laslett 'Mean household size in England since the sixteenth century in Laslett, *Household and Family in Past Time* (Cambridge, 1972).

24 See, Alan Everitt, *Change in the Provinces: The Seventeenth Century* (Leicester, 1972), table II, p. 55.

25 For the hearth tax returns evidence See W.G. Hoskins,

Local History in England (3rd edn, 1984), pp. 278–9. For data that puts Manchester higher on the urban ranking see E.A. Wrigley 'Urban growth and agricultural change' in P. Borsay (ed.), *The Eighteenth-century Town. A reader in English Urban History, 1688–1820* (1990), esp. table 1., pp. 42–3.

26 See S. Bowd, 'John Dee and Christopher Saxton's survey of Manchester (1596)', *Northern History*, xlii (2005), pp. 275–92; J. Lee, *Maps and Plans of Manchester and Salford* (1957), pp.11, 17–18; W.H. Thomson, *History of Manchester to 1852* (Manchester, 1967, pp. 120–4. G. Timmins essay in A. Kidd and T. Wyke, *Manchester: Making the Modern City* (Liverpool, 2016), pp. 41–2.

27 M. Nevell, *From Farmer to Factory Owner: archaeological approaches to the industrial revolution in north-west England* (Manchester, 2003), pp. 32–3.

28 G. Timmins, *Made in Lancashire: A History of Regional Industrialisation* (Manchester, 1998), table 3.4, p. 73.

29 Arthur Trevor to the Marquis of Ormonde, quoted in R.C. Richardson, *Puritanism in North West England* (Manchester, 1972), p. 13.

Chapter 4: 'The greatest mere village in England': roots of industrial revolution, 1660–1780

1 For estimates of Lancashire's population see Phillips and Smith, *Lancashire and Cheshire from AD 1540*, table 1.1, p. 7; M. Daunton, 'Towns and economic growth in eighteenth-century England', table 1, p. 247 in P. Abrams and E.A. Wrigley, *Towns in Societies* (Cambridge, 1978); E.A. Wrigley, 'English county populations in the later eighteenth century', *Economic History Review*, 60 (2007), table 5, pp. 54–5; P. Langford, *A Polite and Commercial People: England, 1727–1783* (Oxford, 1998), p. 673. For Manchester's ranking in the urban hierarchy see Appendix I in W.G. Hoskins, *Local History in England* (Longman: 3rd edn, 1984); E.A. Wrigley, 'Urban growth and agricultural change', in P. Borsay, *The Eighteenth-century Town* (1990); J. Stobart 'An eighteenth-century revolution? Investigating urban growth in North-west England, 1664–1801', *Urban History*, 23 (1996), p. 39, table 2.

2 This was the first census of Manchester's population and deserves wider attention. The original hand-written manuscript is in the Chetham's Library but for a summary see T. Percival, 'Observations on the state of the population of Manchester and other adjacent places', *Proceedings of the Royal Society of London* (1774). For historians' discussions of the evidence for Manchester's eighteenth-century population see Wadsworth and Mann, *The Cotton Trade and Industrial Lancashire*, pp. 509–11; Phillips and Smith, *Lancashire and Cheshire from AD 1540*, pp. 66–8; Nevell, *Manchester: Hidden History*, pp. 65–7; G. Timmins in Chapter 1 of A. Kidd and T. Wyke, *Manchester: Making the Modern City* (Liverpool, 2016). Timmins uses the registers of Manchester Collegiate Church to show that baptisms did not exceed burials until the 1730s suggesting a halting population growth until then.

3 J. Stobart, *The First Industrial Region: North-west England c.1700–60* (Manchester, 2004), esp. pp. 66–71, 75, 94–5, and tables 3.3, 4.2 and figure 4.1.

4 For a discussion of the concept see P. Hudson, *The Industrial Revolution* (1992), ch. 4. For its relevance to Lancashire see Timmins, *Made in Lancashire*, ch. 3; J.K. Walton 'Proto-industrialisation and the first industrial revolution: the case of Lancashire' in P. Hudson (ed.), *Regions and Industries: a perspective on the industrial revolution in England* (Cambridge, 1989).

5 Wadsworth and Mann, *Cotton Trade and Industrial Lancashire*, p. 105. Timmins, *Made in Lancashire*, pp. 78–9.

6 See Stobart, *First Industrial Region*, figs 4.8, 4.9.

7 See M.M. Edwards, *The Growth of the British Cotton Trade, 1780–1815* (Manchester, 1967), esp. pp. 94 and 107.

8 Daniel Defoe, *A Tour Through the Whole Island of Great Britain* (1726; Penguin edn, 1971), pp. 544–5. Compare this with Stukeley's similar observation in the same year: 'Manchester ... the largest, most rich, populous, and busy village in England', William Stukeley, *Itinerarium Curiosum: Or, An Account of the Antiquities, and Remarkable Curiosities in Nature or Art, Observed in Travels through Great Britain* (2nd edn, 1776), p. 58.

9 James Ogden, *A Description of Manchester ... by a Native of the Town* (1783), pp. 93–4. The broadside of 1731 is cited in C. Horner, '"Proper Persons to Deal with": Identification and Attitudes of Middling Society in Manchester, c.1730–c.1760' (unpublished Ph.D. thesis, Manchester Metropolitan University, 2001) p. 75. Lord Kinnoull is quoted in Roy Porter, *English Society in the Eighteenth Century* (1982), p. 215.

10 Wadsworth and Mann, *The Cotton Trade and Industrial Lancashire*, pp. 98–106.

11 See P. Corfield, *The Impact of English Towns, 1700–1800* (Oxford, 1982), pp. 91–3.

12 Horner, 'Proper Persons to Deal with', pp. 69–70, 74, 91, 268.

13 Wadsworth and Mann, *The Cotton Trade and Industrial Lancashire*, pp. 170–2; Edwards, *Growth of British Cotton Trade*, p. 5; M. Rose, *The Lancashire Cotton Industry: a history since 1700* (Preston, 1996), pp. 2-3; H. Hamilton, *An Economic History of Scotland in the Eighteenth Century* (Oxford, 1963), pp. 160–84.

14 Wadsworth and Mann, *The Cotton Trade and Industrial Lancashire*, chs 6, 7; B. Lemire, *Fashion's Favourite: the cotton trade and the consumer in Britain, 1660–1800* (Oxford, 1991), ch. 1.

15 Wadsworth and Mann, *The Cotton Trade and Industrial Lancashire*, pp. 174–5.

16 Lemire, *Fashion's Favourite*, pp. 92–3; Wadsworth and Mann, *The Cotton Trade and Industrial Lancashire*, pp. 173–4.

17 See R.S. Fitton, *The Arkwrights: spinners of fortune* (Manchester, 1989).

18 For an excellent summary of technological change in the cotton industry see G. Timmins' chapter in Rose, *Lancashire Cotton Industry*.

19 R.C. Allen, *The British Industrial Revolution in Global Perspective* (Cambridge, 2009), chs 2, 6. The interventionist French government actively promoted jennies, but they were ignored by the cotton trade. In 1790 France had less than 5 per cent of the number in England. For French knowledge of the jenny see ibid., p. 193. Allen's view on the wage gap between India and Europe has not gone unchallenged. See for example, P. Parthasarathi, *Why Europe grew rich and Asia did not: global economic divergence, 1600–1850* (Cambridge, 2011), pp. 37–46.

20 See Edwards, *Growth of the British Cotton Trade*, pp. 40, 51.

21 P. Langford, *A Polite and Commercial People: England, 1727–1783* (BCA edition, 1999), pp. 402–3, table 5(b).

22 J. Aikin, *A Description of the Country from Thirty to Forty Miles Round Manchester* (1795; repr. David & Charles: Newton Abbot, 1968), p. 184.

23 Alan Kidd, 'Touchet, Samuel (c.1705–1773)', *Oxford Dictionary of National Biography*, (Oxford: Oxford University Press, 2004), www.oxforddnb.com/view/article/57578.

24 For the Hibberts see, K. Donington, *The Bonds of Family: slavery, commerce and culture in the British Atlantic world*, (Manchester, 2020).

25 See E. Williams, *British Capitalism and British Slavery*, (Diasporic Africa Press edition, 2013), originally published in 1944; J. Inikori, *Africans and the Industrial Revolution in England: a study of international trade and economic development* (Cambridge, 2002). For the treatment of this argument in more general studies see S. Beckert, *Empire of Cotton: a global history*, (New York, 2014) and G. Riello, *Cotton: the fabric that made the modern world*, (Cambridge, 2013).

26 Beckert, *Empire of Cotton*, p.87.

27 Edwards, *Growth of the British Cotton Trade*, p. 243.

28 Riello, *Cotton: the fabric that made the modern world*, pp. 138-9.

29 Ibid., chapter 7.

30 See table on p.146, Wadsworth and Mann, *The Cotton Trade and Industrial Lancashire*.

31 P. Maw, 'Yorkshire and Lancashire ascendant: England's textile exports to New York and Philadelphia, 1750-1805', *Economic History Review*, 63(2010), pp. 734-68.

32 Rose, *Lancashire Cotton Industry*, p. 9, table 1:2.

Chapter 5: Living in eighteenth-century Manchester

1 *Through England on a Side Saddle in the time of William and Mary, Being the Diary of Celia Fiennes* (1888), p. 186.

2 See *Historical Maps of Manchester: maps from the eighteenth century*, Digital Archives Association cd-rom (2005), introduction by Terry Wyke. T.Wyke, B.Robson, M.Dodge, *Manchester: Mapping the City* (Edinburgh, 2018) esp. pp. 5–7.

3 See C. Hartwell, *Manchester* (Pevsner Architectural Guides, 2001), p. 253. A tour of the town as it was in the 1750s can be found in F.A. Bruton, *History of Manchester & Salford* (2nd edn, 1927), ch. 21.

4 *Court Leet Records of the Manor of Manchester* (CLR), vol. VII, pp. 49, 122, 228.

5 J.L. Hodgkinson and R. Pogson, *The Early Manchester Theatre* (1960), p.6; R.H. Hills, *Power in the Industrial Revolution* (1970), p. 56; Wadsworth and Mann, *The Cotton Trade and Industrial Lancashire*, p. 475.

6 P. Borsay, *The English Urban Renaissance: culture and society in the provincial town, 1660–1770* (Oxford, 1989), pp. 44–5.

7 Aikin, *Country from Thirty to Forty Miles Round Manchester*, p. 192; for residential divisions within the town see Horner, 'Proper Persons to Deal with', pp. 65-73.

8 Wadsworth and Mann, *The Cotton Trade and Industrial Lancashire*, pp. 358–60.

9 *Manchester Mercury*, 21 June 1757, reproduced in *The Constables' Accounts of the Manor of Manchester* edited by J.P. Earwaker (1892), vol. III, Appendix III. Hadfield may have obtained a *de facto* monopoly of mills and flour shops in the vicinity, see Aikin, *Country from Thirty to Forty Miles Round Manchester*, p. 203. See also F. Nicholson and E. Axon, 'The Hadfield family of Manchester and the food riots of 1757 and 1812', *Transactions of the Lancashire & Cheshire Antiquarian Society*, xxviii (1910–11) pp. 83–90; E.P. Thompson, 'The moral economy of the English crowd in the eighteenth century', *Past and Present*, 50 (1971), pp. 76–136.

10 John Collier wrote under the pseudonym Tim Bobbin. For the 1757 riots see *Whitworth's Manchester Advertiser*, 15, 22 November 1757 reproduced in *Constables' Accounts*, vol. III, Appendix IV. For the rioting in 1750 see *Manchester Magazine*, 11 September 1750, 9 April 1751, cited in Horner, 'Proper Persons to Deal with', pp. 218–19.

11 *Constables' Accounts*, vol. III, pp. 161, 162–3; *Manchester Mercury*, 20 July 1762, reproduced in ibid., Appendix V.

12 Thomas Percival, *Letter to a Friend occasioned by the late Disputes betwixt the Check-makers of Manchester and their Weavers*, quoted in Wadsworth and Mann, *The Cotton Trade and Industrial Lancashire*, p. 362.

13 See H. Barker, *The Business of Women: female enterprise and urban development in northern England, 1760–1830* (Oxford, 2006), esp. tables 2.2, 2.4.

14 Aikin, *Country from Thirty to Forty Miles Round Manchester*, p. 187.

15 Hodgkinson and Pogson, *Early Theatre in Manchester*, pp. 5–14; T. Wyke and N. Rudyard, *Manchester Theatres* (Manchester, 1994), pp. 41–2.

16 This and following paragraphs on societies and sports in Manchester draws on Horner, 'Proper Persons to Deal with', esp. pp. 138-44.

17 *CLR*, vol. VIII, p. 103.

18 For newspapers, publishing and the book trade in eighteenth-century Manchester see *Printing and the Book in Manchester, 1700–1850*, Lancashire & Cheshire Antiquarian Society (2001), essays by Isaac, Horner, Ramwell and Evans; T. Swindells, *Manchester Streets and Manchester Men, Third Series* (Manchester, 1907), pp. 191–202; G.R. Axon, *The Manchester Press before 1801: a list of books, pamphlets and broadsides printed in Manchester in the 18th century* (Manchester Libraries Committee, 1931); C. Horner (ed.), *The Diary of Edmund Harrold, Wigmaker of Manchester, 1712–15* (2008).

19 Cited in *Printing and the Book in Manchester*, essay by Horner, p. 62.

20 See P.K. Monod, *Jacobitism and the English People* (Cambridge, 1989), p. 185; Kazuhiko Kondo, 'Lost in translation: documents relating to the disturbances at Manchester, 1715', in Horner (ed.), *Early Modern Manchester*.

21 For religious and political divisions in Manchester and the events of 1715 and 1745 see Horner, 'Proper Persons to Deal with', ch. 6; Monod, *Jacobitism*, esp. Part Three; Evelyn Lord, *The Stuart's Secret Army: English Jacobites, 1689–1752* (2004); *Constables' Accounts*, vol. III; R. Parkinson (ed.), *The Private Journal and Literary Remains of John Byrom*, vol. II pt 2, Chetham Society (1857); *Victoria County History of Lancaster*, vol. 4 (1911), pp. 174–87; Robert Halley, *Lancashire: Its Puritanism and Nonconformity* (Manchester, 1869), vol II, ch. 8.

22 *Manchester Mercury*, 14 April 1752, cited in Horner, 'Proper Persons to Deal with', pp. 213–14.

23 Linda Colley, *Britons: Forging the Nation, 1707–1837* (1992), pp. 87–8.

24 Aikin, *Country from Thirty to Forty Miles Round Manchester*, p. 112.

25 Ogden, *A Description of Manchester*, p. 3.

Index

Acres Field 28, 84
Adams, Roger 104, 105, 106
Aethelflaed, Lady of the Mercians 16
Africa 73, 78, 79–80
Agricola 5
Aiken, John 92, 113
Alfred the Great 15, 16
'Angel Stone' 16
Anglo-Saxon Chronicle 15, 16
Ardwick Green 93
Arkwright, Richard 70, 73, 74
Ashton-under-Lyne 17, 18, 44, 94

Bakewell 16
Barbados 79
Bath 77
Bayley, James 77
Berry, John 59
Birmingham 61, 62, 66, 97, 106
Blackburn 41, 63
Bland, Ann (*née* Mosley) 105, 107
Bolton 35, 39, 41, 56, 63
book-selling, publishing 105–6
Booth family 55
Booth, Humphrey 43, 47, 52
Booth, Robert 43
boroughreeve 27–8, 45
Bramall, George, corn factor 93, 94, 95
Brazil 79
Bridgewater Canal 5, 89, 113–4
Brigantes, Brigantia 4–6, 9
Bristol 39, 62, 77, 89
Brown Street 84, 100
Buck, Samuel & Nathaniel 83
burgage plots 25, 33, 59, 83

Bury 39, 63
Byrom family 60, 77, 85, 88, 91, 102
Byrom John 77, 79, 88, 97, 106, 110, 112, 113
Byrom Street 85, 90

Camden, William 38
canals 85, 89, 113–4
Carlisle 3, 109, 111, 112
Cartimandua 5
Casson & Berry maps 49, 59, 83, 85, 86–7, 89, 91, 103
castle at Manchester 19–20, 22 (see also manor house)
Castlefield 1, 3, 6, 114
Chapel Street, Salford 99
Charles I 56
Charles II 58
Charter of 1301 22, 27, 28 (see also Manchester, manor of)
checks 65, 70, 73
Cheshire 3, 5, 35, 44, 56, 63, 65, 96, 105
Chester 3, 16, 34, 39, 55, 58, 62, 77
Chetham family 41, 43–4, 60, 77
Chetham, George 41, 43
Chetham, Humphrey 26, 42, 43, 44, 45
Chetham's College (Hospital, Library) 19, 24, 26, 42, 43, 44
Christ's College (college of priests) 24, 26, 30, 31, 37, 63, (see also Warre, Thomas de la, collegiate church)
Clarkson, Thomas 80

Clowes, Samuel 85
'Cobden House' 85, 91
cockfighting 103–4
Collegiate Church (see also Christ's College, Manchester Cathedral) 26, 27, 30, 31, 51, 85, 87, 92, 107–8, 111
Collier, John (Tim Bobbin) 93, 94–5, 106
Collyhurst, sandstone quarries 24, 84, plague pits 54
Cornovii 5
cotton manufacture & trade 41, 42, 61, 63, 64, 65–6, 69–77, 78–81, 84, 114, 115
Court Leet 35, 44–51, 57–8, 59, 66, 89, 90, 103, 104
Coventry 68
Cromwell, Oliver 58
Crompton, Samuel (spinning mule) 73
Cross Street Chapel 78, 107, 108–9

Deansgate 3, 5, 16, 19, 23, 25, 37, 51, 57, 59, 77, 84, 103
Derby 105, 111
Derbyshire 4, 46, 70, 74
Dee, John 37, 59
Domesday Book 17
Dublin 16

East India Company 71, 73, 76
Edward the Elder, king of Wessex 15, 16, 18
Elizabeth I 41, 59
English Civil War 35, 55–7

Fennel Street 99
Fiennes, Celia 82
Flemish weavers 29, 32
food riots 92–6
food supply 47–8, 49–50, 92, 95–6
Fountain Street 50
France, French cotton industry 75
fustians, fustian trade 41, 42–3, 44, 47, 52, 60, 61, 63, 64, 65, 66, 70

George III 86
Glasgow 70
Gresle (Grelley) family 18, 20
Gresle, Albert de 18
Gresle Robert de 20
Gresle Thomas de 22, 27
guilds, absence of 66–7, 68

Hadrian's Wall 3, 4
Hanging Bridge 23
Hanging Ditch 23, 29, 32, 36, 51, 60
Hargreaves, James (spinning jenny) 73, 75, 76
Harrold, Edmund 106
Harrop, Joseph 104, 105, 106 (see also *Manchester Mercury*)
Hastings, battle of 18
Heape, Thomas 41
Heaton Norris 17, 18
Henry VIII 26
Hibbert family 78, 80, 81
Hibbert, Thomas 78, 80
High, Thomas 90
Holy Trinity Church, Salford 85
Holt, George 40, 41
horseracing 102–3
Hunts Bank 57, 85
Hull 34, 43

India, Indian cottons 69, 71, 73, 75, 80 (see also East India Company)
industrial revolution, concept of 63–4
Ireland 16, 38, 46
Irk, River 3, 17, 19, 20, 22, 23, 29
Irwell, River 3, 5, 17, 19, 20, 24, 25, 37, 45, 50, 85

Jacobite 'Pretenders', Jacobitism 2, 82, 88, 107, 108–12, 113
Jamaica 78, 79, 80
John Berry's Long Room 105
John Shaw's Punch House 98, 102
John Street 85

Kay, John (flying shuttle) 73, 75
Kendal 38
Kenyon, George 85
Kersal 44
Kersal Moor 102
King Street 84, 86, 88, 90, 92, 100

Lancashire 18, 26, 33, 39, 52, 55, 56, 57, 58, 62, 63, 70, 96
Lancaster 20
Leeds 61, 68, 106
Leicester 61
Leigh 63
Leland, John 36, 39
Levant, The 78, 79
Levant Company 41–2
linen industry 38–9, 41, 61, 63, 64, 65, 69
Liverpool 20, 26, 35, 62, 68, 76, 77, 89, 97
Locker, Francis 41
London 29, 39, 40, 41–2, 44, 49, 55, 62, 66, 69, 70, 78, 81, 105
Long Millgate 23, 25, 37, 55, 57, 59, 92

Macclesfield 35
Magna Carta 20
Mainwaring, Peter, physician 88
'Manchester Act' (1736) 73
Manchester Cathedral 3, 16, 23, 26, 30–1 (see also collegiate church)
'Manchester Cottons' 38–9
Manchester Exchange (1729) 88, 89, 90, 97, 100, 109, 112
Manchester Grammar School 36–7
Manchester Infirmary 88, 102, 103, 112
Manchester Literary & Philosophical Society 88

Manchester, manor of, manorial borough 18, 19, 20–2, 24, 25, 26–8, 41, 45, 66 (see also Charter of 1301, Court Leet)
Manchester Mercury, newspaper 94, 100, 103, 104–5 (see also Joseph Harrop)
Manchester, parish of, parish church 17, 21, 22, 25, 26, 33, 60
'Manchester Regiment' 107, 111
'Manchester Word Square' 11, 13
manor house 20, 22, 24, 25, 26 (see also Christ's College, Chetham's College)
Market Place 23, 46, 48, 54–5, 77, 88, 97, 99, 104
markets 46–50, 59, 89–90, 103, 112
Market Street 23, 25, 37, 49, 57, 59, 84, 93, 103, 111
Marsden Street 100
Medlock, River 3, 5, 8, 9, 10, 11, 14
merchant clothiers 38–9, 40–3, 64
Mersey, River 16, 18, 85
Mersey & Irwell Navigation 85, 89
military operations: Roman conquest 5–6, Saxon refortification 15–16, English Civil War 55–7, food riots 92, 94–5, Jacobite risings 107, 108–12
Mithras, mithraism 8, 13–15
Mosley family 18, 40, 55, 77, 107
Mosley, Anthony 40–1
Mosley, Edward 57
Mosley, Nicholas 40–1, 55
Mosley, Oswald 85, 88, 103
Mosley Street 100

Nantes 75
Newcastle 77
newspapers 104–5, 110 (see also *Manchester Mercury*)
Northumbria 15, 18
Norwich 29, 33, 62, 77
Nottingham 61

Ogden, James 66, 114
Oldham 41
Oldham, Hugh 36

Ottoman Empire 78
Oxford 77

Parsonage, Parsonage Gardens 25, 85
Paul, Lewis 78
Percival, Thomas 96–7, 107
plague 35, 41, 52, 54–5
Poitou, Roger de 18
population 34–5, 58–9, 62–3, 66
poverty, poor relief 51, 52–5, 57
Preston 20, 35, 39, 109, 111

Quay Street 85–6, 91

Raffald, Elizabeth 97, 98, 99–100, 106
Rhuddlan 16
Ribble, River 18, 19
Rochdale 48, 63
Rochdale Canal 5, 89
Rosworm, John 56–7
Rouen 75

Saint-Domingue 79
Salford 17, 18, 24, 28, 40, 52, 57, 58, 62, 63, 85, 99
Salford Hundred 18,19, 28, 48, 56
St Ann's church 84, 85, 107
St Ann's Square 50, 84, 85–6, 90, 92, 100
St Ann's Passage 100
St James's Square 84

St Mary's Gate 49
sanitation, water supply 37, 50–1
Saxton, Christopher 59
Setantii 5
Shambles, Wellington Inn 49, 53, 59–60, 77, 85, 90
Sheffield 61
Shropshire 5
Shude Hill 59, 94
'Shude Hill Fight' 94–5
silk, silk industry, 65, 70, 71, 72, 73, 77, 96
slavery, slave trade, slave ownership 76–7, 78–81
smallwares 41, 65, 70, 96, 97
Smithy Door 49, 55
Spinningfields 85
Spring Gardens 50, 101
Stanley, Edward 11th Earl of Derby 110
Stanley, William, 6th Earl of Derby 56
Stanley, James, 7th Earl of Derby 56, 57
Stockport 35, 63
strikes 96–7

Tacitus 5
textile industries, trade 60, 61, 63, 64–6, 68, 69, 70–1, 73–5, 80, 89 (see also cotton, checks, fustians, linen, silk, smallwares, wool)
theatre, theatrical performances 90, 97, 100, 101
Touchet family 77–8, 80
Touchet, Samuel 78

United States of America 76, 79, 81

Venetius 5
vikings 15, 16

Warre, Thomas de la 24, 26
Warrington 28, 48, 85
Water Street 85
Wellington Inn 53, 59–60 (see also Shambles)
West Indies 78–9 (see also Barbados, Jamaica, Saint Domingue)
Whitworth, Robert 83, 85,104,105–6, 110
Wigan 4, 20, 26, 58, 111
William the Conqueror 17, 18
Withington 18, 94
Withy Grove 37, 59
wool, woollen industry 29, 32, 33, 38–9, 40, 41, 63, 64, 65, 69, 71

York 3, 8, 16, 18, 62, 77
Yorkshire 46, 55,105
York Street 101